THE
ENGLISH LANGUAGE

THE
ENGLISH LANGUAGE

by

C. L. Wrenn

LONDON

METHUEN & CO LTD

First published on 22 September 1949
Reprinted with minor corrections 1952
Reprinted nine times

First published as a University Paperback in 1977
by Methuen & Co Ltd, 11 New Fetter Lane
London EC4P 4EE

Printed in Great Britain
at the
University Printing House, Cambridge

ISBN 0 416 85810 4

Distributed in the U.S.A. by

HARPER & ROW PUBLISHERS, INC.
BARNES & NOBLE IMPORT DIVISION

CONTENTS

CHAPTER   PAGE

I. INTRODUCTION   1
   1. General Considerations
   2. General Character of English
   3. The Indo-European Family of Languages
   4. The Germanic Family
   5. English in the Germanic Family
   6. Landmarks in the History of English
   7. Philology and Literature

II. VOCABULARY   33
   1. General Remarks
   2. The Influences of Latin
   3. Greek Influence
   4. French Influences on the Vocabulary
   5. Scandinavian Elements
   6. Other Germanic Languages
   7. The Influence of Italy
   8. Other European Influences
   9. Words from Outside of Europe
   10. Recent and Current Tendencies

III. SPELLING AND PRONUNCIATION   85
   1. General Considerations
   2. History of Spelling and Pronunciation
   3. 'Standardizing' of Spelling and Pronunciation
   4. The Development of Dictionaries
   5. Spelling and Rhyme
   6. Influence of Spelling on Pronunciation

IV. THE SHAPING, BUILDING AND ORDERING
       OF WORDS. I   106
   1. General Considerations
   2. The Shapes and Ends of Words
   3. The Englishing of Foreign Words
   4. Word-building
   5. The Influence of Dialects
   6. Development in Word-Meanings
   7. Homophones and Homonyms
   8. Archaism

vii

CHAPTER	PAGE
V. THE SHAPING, BUILDING AND ORDERING OF WORDS. II	130
1. The Ordering of Words and Syntax	
2. Syntax and Parts of Speech	
3. Intonation	
VI. INDIVIDUALS AND THE MAKING OF MODERN ENGLISH	146
1. General Considerations	
2. Bible Translations	
3. Shakespeare's Influence	
4. Some Formative Working Critics	
5. Milton and the English Language	
6. Some Poets and the Language	
7. Rhetoric and Oratory	
VII. THE ENGLISH LANGUAGE TO-DAY	185
1. General Considerations	
2. The Search for a Standard	
3. American Influence	
4. The Radio and the Language	
5. Other Influences on English	
6. English as a World Language	
VIII. AIMS AND METHODS OF STUDY	206
1. General Considerations	
2. Methods of Study	
3. Some English Language Studies of the Past	
4. Select Bibliography	
SUBJECT INDEX	225
WORD INDEX	228

CHAPTER I

INTRODUCTION

I. GENERAL CONSIDERATIONS

LANGUAGE is the expression of human personality in words, whether written or spoken. It is the universal medium alike for conveying the common facts and feelings of everyday life and the philosophers' searchings after truth, and all that lies between. Like any other way of expressing the human mind, it must, by the very nature of its being, be both inaccurate and incomplete: and for this reason some modern philosophers have doubted its validity or usefulness for the attempt to convey any kind of truth other than that which pertains to material things. Yet thinkers as well as poets have always assumed that language can be the bearer of all kinds of truth and the imager of every sort of reality; nor can mathematical or other scientific symbols take the place of language among any but a highly technical group of specialists: and even these will probably only manage to substitute one unfamiliar and equally inaccurate series of signs for the shortcomings of that most intimately known and felt complex of verbal signs which is language. It will be taken for granted, therefore, in what follows that language as defined above is the normal, natural and enduring method of expressing the human mind which is the nearest to universal.

But because of its universality and the consequent almost limitless variety of its uses, language may be looked at in many distinct ways; and no book which pretends to treat of this subject can avoid confining itself to only a comparatively small and select portion of these uses.

For instance, language may be thought of in general terms, as opposed to the particular words of a given speaker or writer in a known context: or a particular language may be considered either as one learns of it through grammars and dictionaries and textbooks, or as it is encountered in a special situation, a known speaker and a remembered occasion. From this standpoint, the one has been termed 'language', and the other 'speech'. 'Language', then would mean both language in general and any particular language considered quite apart from any actual speaker or situation: 'speech' would mean the words used by some individual in a more or less precisely known situation or context. Or again, this distinction between 'language' and 'speech' has been drawn in a slightly different way by some scholars as a difference between the 'outer' and the 'inner' language. The 'outer' language is speech or writing as we view it from the outside, without consciousness of any particular individual or situation; while the 'inner' language is that of a particular speaker or writer in a set of known circumstances or in a given context. One might say, quite broadly, that 'language' or 'outer' language is viewed from the outside, while 'speech' or 'inner' language is seen or heard from the inside—from an actual human being as distinct from merely assumed groups or types of speakers. Thus it may be said that the French *cheval*, the Italian *cavallo* and the Russian *kon'* all mean 'horse' and that this is a fact of 'language' and of 'outer' language: for the French, Italians and Russians all share a common body of intuited knowledge with the British, and the words for 'horse' can be interchanged in translating from one of their languages into another. But when one remembers how differently this same general notion of 'horse' is inwardly felt and apprehended by different nations—how differently the Frenchman, Italian, Russian and Englishman *feel* towards this animal, one can see that from the standpoint of the 'speech' or 'inner' language, the four words cited for 'horse' are not really interchangeable in translation at all. And if we were to carry the illustration farther afield to countries in Asia or Africa, we should find the differences in the 'inner' language about the horse were far more marked. Clearly, however, such distinctions are only to be employed when one is dealing with the more specialized and technical aspects of language: and in this book—which seeks only to present a general conspectus of the more important facts about the English language—we must confine our study for the most part to 'language' or 'outer' language. Yet the distinctions should never be forgotten.

Another recent approach to the study of language has sought to divide it into 'indicative', that is the language used to state facts, and the 'emotive', the language which seeks to arouse feeling or suggest an emotional attitude. From this standpoint, the 'emotive' language is often held to have no real meaning as an expression of truth. Indeed Shelley's famous lines

'Life, like a dome of many-coloured glass,
Stains the white radiance of eternity,'

have been held to be meaningless except for their emotional suggestion. But it is only on the assumption that there is no truth beyond the purely material world that the 'emotive' type of language can be wholly rejected as a possible vehicle of truth: and as has been said already, poets as well as thinkers have usually been supported in a normal and natural way in their assumption that what they say or write may be the valid expression of something real or true. In other words, the distinction between the 'indicative' and the 'emotive' in language is one which over-simplifies and may mislead: for there may be factual matter conveyed emotively, just as there may be meaningless statements made in apparently 'indicative' language. We shall not, therefore, observe at all this kind of distinction in this book, though most of the account of the English language in so brief a compass is likely naturally to treat of 'indicative' language. But the work of great poets like Shakespeare and Milton, who have left by their influence some permanent imprint upon the language, must not be left out of the account in any balanced study of the language as a whole. A possible third type of language which might be added to the 'indicative' and the 'emotive', is what may be termed the 'symbolic'. Since language has come into existence mainly as the needed means of expressing material facts and conveying information about the material world, it follows naturally that such reality or truth as may be outside our experience of the world of phenomena or matter, should find its expression in the form of symbols which describe, for instance, spiritual things which are beyond physical observation by symbols which liken them to the most comparable things in our phenomenal world. Now when this is done without indicating that a comparison is being made, when the things of this world are merely being used as substitutes or symbols of realities outside the sphere for the description of which language has grown up, the resulting language may properly be called 'symbolic'. Goethe, for example, in his drama *Faust*, has made a character exclaim that 'All theory is grey, and the golden tree of life is green'. The meaning of this is quite clear, though the words used are almost entirely symbolic. This aspect of language will, naturally, only appear incidentally in what follows.

Nothing is known for certain, though very much has been speculated, of the origin of language. This is partly because thought and language cannot clearly be separated, since the one can scarcely seem to exist without the other. Therefore the origin of language seems to be bound up with that of human thought. We must decide when and how man began to think, to know of the beginnings of language; and we must know when and how he began to speak, to decide on the origins of his existence as a thinking being. The Greeks implied and included in their word *logos* both the power of speech (what the Latins termed *oratio*) and that of thought (the Latin *ratio*): and in St. John's statement at the opening of his Gospel that 'In the beginning was the *word*' (the Greek *logos*), he may be held to have indicated that in the mind of God there co-existed from the beginning thought and language. The theory of the evolution of man as known to scientists, then, must find a place for the emergence of man as a possessor of language as distinct from the so-called 'highest' species of anthropoid apes whose varied cries are not language (which implies thought), but only very fully developed conditioned reflexes.

The gap between the highest anthropoid ape and the most 'primitive' man has not yet been bridged from this point of view of the emergence of language in what may be called 'homo loquens', which is really the same thing as the familiar 'homo sapiens'. The hypothesis of some kind of creative act, therefore, may still be tenable in default of a better in considering the origin of language.

2. GENERAL CHARACTER OF ENGLISH

The English language is spoken or read by the largest number of people in the world, for historical, political and economic reasons; but it may also be true that it owes something of its wide appeal to qualities and characteristics inherent in itself. What are these characteristic features which outstand in making the English language what it is, which give it its individuality and make it of this world-wide significance? Some of the more obvious of these are the following. First and most important is its extraordinary receptive and adaptable heterogeneousness —the varied ease and readiness with which it has taken to itself material from almost everywhere in the world and has made the new elements of language its own. English, which when the Anglo-Saxons first conquered England in the fifth and sixth centuries was almost a 'pure' or unmixed language—which could make new words for new ideas from its own compounded elements and had hardly any foreign words—has become the most 'mixed' of languages, having received throughout its history all kinds of foreign elements with ease and assimilated them all to its own character. Though its copiousness of vocabulary is outstanding, it is its amazing variety and heterogeneousness which is even more striking: and this general receptiveness of new elements has contributed to making it a suitable and attractive vehicle in so many parts of the world.

A second outstanding characteristic of English is its simplicity of inflexion—the ease with which it indicates the relationship of words in a sentence with only the minimum of change in their shapes or variation of endings. There are languages such as Chinese, that have surpassed English in the reduction of the language in the matter of inflexions to what looks like just a series of fixed monosyllabic roots: but among European languages, taken as a whole, English has gone as far as any in reducing the inflexions it once had to a minimum. A natural consequence of this simplifying of inflexion by reduction, however, is that since the relationship of words to each other is no longer made clear by their endings, this must be done in other ways.

A third quality of English, therefore, is its relatively fixed word-order. An inflected language like Latin or Russian can afford to be fairly free in the arrangement of its words, since the inflexions shew clearly the proper relationship in the sentence, and ambiguity is unlikely. But in a language which does not change the forms of its words according to their relationship in the sentence-significance, the order of the words is likely to be relatively fixed; and a fixed word-order in relation to meaning in the sentence takes the place of the freedom made possible by the system of inflexions.

Another consequence, fourthly, of the loss or reduction to the minimum of the inflexions which English once had, is the growth of the use of periphrases or roundabout ways of saying things, and of the use of prepositions to take the place of the lost inflexions. The English simplified verb uses periphrases and compound tenses made with auxiliary verbs to replace the more elaborate system of tenses that once existed (though tenses had already become fairly simple before the Anglo-Saxons came to England). Similarly, English, which once had nearly as many case-endings as Latin, has come to use prepositions instead of these, as can easily be seen if one translates any piece of Latin into English.

A fifth quality of English—though this, like the loss of inflexions and its consequences is shared with some other languages—is the development of new varieties of intonation to express shades of meaning which were formerly indicated by varying the shapes of words. This is perhaps somewhat comparable (though only in a small way) to the vast use of intonation in Chinese as a method of expressing meaning in sentences which would otherwise seem like series of unvarying monosyllabic roots. Consider, for instance, the wonderful variety of shades of meaning we may put into the use of the word 'do', merely by varying the intonation—that is the pitch and intensity, the tone of the voice.

Not all the above qualities are in themselves necessarily good, nor have they all contributed to the general success of English. But it seems probable that of them all it is the adaptable receptiveness and the simplicity of inflexion that have done most in this regard. On the other hand, the very copiousness and heterogeneousness of English leads to vagueness or lack of clarity. Its resources are too vast for all but the well educated to use to full advantage; and such phenomena as 'pidgin English', 'journalese', jargon, woolliness of expression and slatternly speech and writing, are everywhere likely to be met with. It may fairly be said that English is among the easiest languages to speak badly, but the most difficult to use well.

What, then, is the place of this English among the world's languages? To what family, so to speak, does it belong? And who are its relations?

3. THE INDO-EUROPEAN FAMILY OF LANGUAGES

If one compares a number of languages, it probably soon appears that some of them have some sort of relationship to one another, while others may seem quite isolated. If then we are able to trace a group of these apparently related forms in several languages to a common ancestor by means of older writings, it may sometimes become almost certain that these forms must be branches, as it were, from a common root. By going further back, we may sometimes be able to compare a number of early forms each of which is the ancestor of later developments in the different languages, so as to establish a strong probability that they in their turn must all be descended from a common prehistoric original. This supposed original will be much older than the earliest written languages, so that it can never be verified with absolute certainty, but must remain only a strongly supported hypothesis. But if other qualities in the languages we are comparing corroborate the relationship and common ancestry which we have arrived at by the above method, we may find ourselves well on the way to being able to construct a genealogy of our languages—in other words to classify them into families. For example, if we take the words for 'is' in some of the better known European and Asiatic languages, we may reconstruct with fair probability the ancestral prehistoric word from which all must be descended: and this relationship will be found to be confirmed by other evidence. Latin *est*, Greek *esti*, Sanskrit *asti*, Russian *est'* [*jest'*], German *ist*, Italian *é*, etc. Now by studying the earliest forms and the later history of each of these languages, we can be pretty sure that the ancestral form from which all descend was **esti*. We know, for instance, that in Sanskrit an original *e*-sound became *a*, and that the Italian pronunciation reduced the earlier Latin *est* to a form indicated by the modern spelling *é*. Thus, such forms as **esti* should always be written with an asterisk to remind all concerned that they are only probable reconstructions of ancestral or primitive forms as distinct from those attested by writing. Though such 'starred forms' are necessary to the speculative specialist in the early history of languages and in classification, for the student who is primarily only dealing with English, it is clear that the fewer of them he uses, the better.

English belongs, in all its stages, to the *Indo-European* family of languages, formerly called *Indo-Germanic*, and still earlier *Aryan*. 'Indo-European' is the name given to the set of linguistic forms from which nearly all European languages as well as those of Persia and a very large part of India can be shewn to have descended. We do not know that all these prehistoric forms co-existed or that they can properly be said to have been collectively an actual language:

for languages and parts of languages change at differing speeds. Nor would it be right to assume that there was necessarily ever a race or people who spoke this Indo-European as their language. Race, culture and language need not always correspond or be coextensive, as may be seen in modern Switzerland.

'Indo-European' is used because it merely suggests that the languages it comprises cover most of Europe and India, or that Europe and India mark the length of its confines. The predominance and pioneering position of the German philologists of the nineteenth century sufficiently accounts for the earlier term 'Indo-Germanic'. 'Aryan' was the name (from the Sanskrit *aryas* 'noble') which the fairer-skinned bringers of the Hindu civilization to India from the North gave themselves to distinguish them from the darker and less cultured peoples whom they largely conquered: and the belief among the predecessors of the more scientific German philologists that Sanskrit, with its remarkably full inflexions, was the ancestor of all the then studied European and Asiatic languages, may explain the use of the term 'Aryan' for what we now call Indo-European.

Beginning at some period several thousand years B.C., this 'Indo-European', starting perhaps at a point in Southern Europe near the Asian border, spread itself both East and West. As it spread, with the changing needs of its speakers for different homes, it mixed with many 'non-Indo-European' tongues and was modified by them variously at different stages. As speakers spread farther and farther from the starting-point, their kinds of Indo-European developed more and more qualities which made them different from their ancestor. In some such way, very broadly, may be described the gradual growth through successive stages of what have become the modern languages of Europe, Persia and India as we know them.

There are eight main groups of Indo-European languages, all traceable back to the Indo-European primitive ancestor. These are divided into roughly an Eastern and a Western set of groups. The Eastern set comprises four groups of languages, which have in common certain basic changes from the original system, such as a general shift in the pronunciation of the so-called 'guttural' consonants *g* and *k* to a 'palatal' position. Thus, for instance, the Indo-European assumed primitive form for the numeral 100 is *kmtóm*: but whereas languages of the Western set of groups such as Latin (*centum*) retain the original *k*-sound, Sanskrit has changed the *k* to an *sh*-sound [ʃ] (*śatám*) and Russian has the word as *sto*. For this reason, the Western languages are commonly referred to as '*Centum*-languages' and the Eastern— after the old Persian or Iranian form of the word—as '*Satem*-languages'. The four Eastern groups are: *Balto-Slavic*—including all the Slavonic tongues ancient and modern and the related languages of Baltic countries such as Lithuania and Latvia; *Indo-Iranian* —including the languages of old and new India of which Sanskrit is the type and of Iran–Persia; then *Armenian* ancient and modern with its various dialects; and finally *Albanian* which is only spoken over a relatively small area but forms a separate group by its nature none the less. The Western groups are *Greek*, ancient and modern with their many dialects, *Latin* and all its derivatives, *Celtic* which survives in ancient inscriptions and in the mediaeval and modern languages of Wales, Ireland, the Scottish Highlands and Brittany, and formerly existed in Cornwall and the Isle of Man; and finally the *Germanic* group, which comprises the languages of Germany, Scandinavia, Holland and the Flemish parts of Belgium as well as English, and includes these in some ancient and mediaeval forms also. It is only with this last, the *Germanic* group, that we are here concerned. But what is it that makes this Germanic, and therefore English, Indo-European?

Indo-European is but one of a number of families into which the world's languages may be divided; and it must be remembered too that there are still many languages, and even whole groups, that have not been examined scientifically or committed to writing yet, and hence cannot be fitted into any scheme of classification. Broadly speaking, it may be said that two outstanding characteristics indicate the 'Indo-Europeanness' of a language; its structure and its vocabulary. Indo-European languages generally lend themselves in structure, at least if one knows something of their historical development, to that description of forms invented by the ancient Greeks and named by them 'Parts of Speech'. A language may have inflexions fully retained relatively from the original Indo-European, like Russian, or it may have lost most of its distinctive word-endings like modern English: it may, as the grammarians say, be 'synthetic' with full inflexions or 'analytic' with few or none. But if we can think of its forms fairly readily as nouns, verbs, etc., that is to say under the traditional classical terms of 'Parts of Speech', it will probably be found to be Indo-European. Chinese, with its forms consisting not of parts of speech, but of what seem now to be merely monosyllabic roots, is therefore not Indo-European. Or again, even in Europe, there are what are called 'Finno-Ugrian' or 'Uralian' languages—Hungarian and Finnish for instance, which do not shew parts of speech, or even words in our ordinary sense always. Here a kind of phrase-complex takes the place of a clause or group of words and all kinds of things can be said about an object by building up a single root with prefixes and suffixes. These languages are sometimes classed as 'agglutinative' or 'incorporating'. Many of the languages of Central Asia now in the U.S.S.R. are of this kind. In the matter of vocabulary, secondly, Indo-European languages have so much in common, namely a shared nucleus of fundamental roots, that this common basis of vocabulary (often changed beyond recognition except by the linguistic specialist) may serve to distinguish them from all others. Thus, for instance, most of the names of family relationships, of elementary domestic materials and of familiar animals, if compared in their historical early forms and traced back to what must have been their pre-written ancestors, can be seen to be shared by the Indo-European languages and not to be found in those forms except by 'borrowing' outside those groups.

Germanic, then, is Indo-European in the sense that it uses the parts of speech, whether with full inflexions synthetically as in its ancient forms, or with reduced inflexions tending towards the analytic, as in modern Dutch or English, and because, secondly, it shares a fundamental nucleus of the vocabulary of the commonest things with other Indo-European tongues. There are other tests which perhaps should be applied: but enough has been said to indicate broadly what is meant by describing English as Indo-European.

4. THE GERMANIC FAMILY

Probably in the millennium preceding the Christian era there grew up in Northern Europe a type of Indo-European from which descended all those languages which we call Germanic. Its forms can only be reconstructed on probabilities by working back from known languages, and it is merely for convenience that it is usually referred to as 'Primitive Germanic'. A better term might be 'Common Germanic', since we do not know for certain that it was ever a language in the full sense of the term, but only that there were a number of prehistoric forms to which the known Germanic languages can be traced back. This Germanic, as we may deduce from its historical and known derivatives, had certain characteristics which distinguish it and all its developments from other Indo-European groups. Apart from those which are mainly of only historical interest to the specialist, two characteristics stand out as marking off, as it were, the Germanic family of languages. These must have existed in 'Primitive' or 'Common' Germanic and go far to account for qualities developed in the historical tongues (Scandinavian, German, Dutch, English and the rest) which belong to this family. They are, first, a strong tendency to fix the stress (weight or emphasis) of a word on its root syllable or as near to its beginning as possible: and secondly the building up of a 'two-tense' system in the verb.

During the centuries immediately before Christ, the *Common Germanic* collection of forms used among tribes of Northern Europe developed within itself separatist tendencies; and with the progress of the migrations of its users into Western and Central Europe, there arose those historical languages from one section of which English is descended. A so-called 'Eastern' group of Germanic languages has only left written monuments in the Gothic translations of the Bible made near the end of the fourth century A.D. But a 'Northern' group has given us the Scandinavian tongues with monuments from almost all periods since the fourth century: and a 'Western' group, to which English belongs, has given us the languages of Germany, Holland, Friesland, Flemish Belgium and England, with historical records which in England, where early monuments are fullest, go back to the seventh century A.D. All of these languages and their dialects shew the common Germanic characteristics of which the most significant two, namely the system of fixed stress and the two-tense verb, have already been mentioned. Let us glance for a moment at these and their effects.

The terms 'stress' and 'accent' are often vaguely used. Generally they may refer to either pitch, that is the height or tone of the voice of the speaker, or the emphasis or force with which the sound is uttered. Using the term 'stress', as already indicated, in the sense of emphasis or force or weight of utterance, we shall keep the term 'accent' for pitch and intonation. Both stress and accent, in these restricted senses, play a great part in languages, and their relative importance varies from one group of tongues to another. Indo-European had functions of importance for both the stress and the musical accent: during its development and before the emergence of separate groups of descending languages, it seems that stress came to dominate. But this stress was free, that is it could be on different parts of the same word according to context and meaning. This free stress has been preserved in some conservative languages such as Russian, for instance, where we have *dom* 'house' as against *domá* 'of a house', or *pis'mó* 'letter' but *pís'ma* 'letters'. Now it is the Germanic language characteristic more than any other group to fix the stress as near as may be to the beginning of the word. Inevitably, as we may hear every day from ordinary speech, the syllables at the end of a word in such a language as puts a strong stress at the beginning, will tend to be first blurred in utterance and finally even lost completely. It is this fixing of the stress near the beginning of a word in the Germanic languages that is the primary cause of the reduction and loss of inflexions which has been so marked a characteristic of English. It is, as has been said, a common Germanic tendency: but its effects in inflexional reduction have been varied in speed among the different Germanic languages, though clearly perceptible in all. It is a mistake, as some have done, to think of this simplifying of inflexions, which is so marked a quality in English, as necessarily anything to do with progress. There are advantages in a fully-inflected language like some of the Slavonic group, which English cannot have, such as the avoidance of ambiguity, for instance. This loss of inflexions, then, is mainly just the natural result which follows from the Germanic fixation of the primary stress, the syllables farthest away from this stress tending to become weak and later to cease to be heard.

Indo-European had an elaborate system of verb-conjugation, in which the multitude of forms, that in historic times came mainly to indicate the time or tense of the action, shewed rather the way the action was thought *of* or looked *at* by the speaker, or its 'aspect' as the grammarians have called it. Thus, for example, one series of forms in the verb shewed the action as continuing or progressing (*durative* aspect); another indicated that it was thought of as quite independent of time (*aorist, punctual* or *momentaneous* aspect); a third meant that the action was considered as presenting a state resulting from an already completed act (*perfective* aspect); while yet a fourth implied that it was being repeated several times (*iterative* aspect). These and many other of what seem to us now refinements and complexities of the verbal system, which survive in some groups of languages fairly fully, as in Greek, have been simplified in varying degrees in different languages. But the outstanding feature of the Germanic verb is that it has properly only two tenses, a present and a past, which are indicated by the primary forms of the verb, the other tenses being shewn by means of auxiliary verbs and compound tenses, etc. Now this extreme simplification of the verb in Germanic has fundamentally affected the character of the languages concerned, resulting not only in a multiplying of compound tenses, but also in a great increase of flexibility of expression, greater subtlety and, at times, in greater opportunities for looseness in the language.

A third characteristic of Germanic, but one which

we need not enlarge on here, is its peculiar development of the two main classes of its verbs into the so-called strong and weak kinds. *Strong* verbs (the term was first used by Jakob Grimm of the *Fairy Tales* who made the first scientific comparative German grammar from 1822) are those which indicate their tense by change of vowel according to regular series, as in the modern forms *drive, drove, driven*. Such series of vowel-variation in relation to change of meaning were called by Grimm *Ablaut*-series and are known in English as vowel-gradations: we see such a gradation in *fĭdus, foedus, fīdes*. But the distinctive feature of Germanic is that it uses such gradations to shew regularly change of tense in the verb, whereas in other languages this is only a less frequent device. But this method of shewing tense by change of vowel in a series was originally only used in primary verbs, that is in those which denoted simple actions and were not merely derived from the forms of other words. Verbs which denote actions derived from other words (such as *to love* from the noun *love*) Grimm called *weak* because they are secondary or derivative and because they do not change their root-vowel in conjugation. Weak verbs, then, are those which are secondary or derived, which shew their tense not by gradation of vowel, but merely by adding something (a suffix ending in *d* or *t*) to their end (such as *love loved*). But this distinction of strong and weak verbs as a Germanic characteristic is less satisfactory, because it has become blurred to some extent through later changes of sound. One might guess, for instance, that Modern English *buy bought* was a strong verb because of the change of vowel: but it is historically a weak verb. Its final *t* reminds us of the dental suffix (*d* or *t*) which is the mark of the weak verb; and by reconstructing through the Gothic forms we can see that in Common Germanic the corresponding types to *buy* and *bought* were **bugjan* and **buhta*, with no change of vowel. It is later sound-changes in various periods that have led to the misleading Modern English forms with differing vowels according to tense. But the point is that this distinction between strong and weak verbs no longer holds good without reservation for the language of to-day, and cannot be safely insisted on.

The *Germani* were properly merely one of the many tribes who afterwards came to be grouped together under the name Germanic (they may even have been in fact Celts speaking a Germanic dialect): but the term, already implicit in the Roman historian Tacitus who wrote his account of *Germania* about A.D. 100, is both in general use and convenient. The older name *Teutonic* for the Germanic languages is still sometimes to be met with.

5. ENGLISH IN THE GERMANIC FAMILY

The earliest period of English was formerly called 'Anglo-Saxon', and the term may still be used: but 'Old English' has tended to replace it with most scholars. But both terms have their drawbacks from the point of view of strict accuracy.

According to Bede, and the *Anglo-Saxon Chronicle* which here is based largely on his early eighth-century work, the tribes which came to settle forcibly and overrun most of Romanized Britain in the fifth and sixth centuries were from parts of Northern Germany and were Angles, Saxons and Jutes. These brought with them what is called a 'Low German' type of language, or rather one which was transplanted to England too early to be affected by the 'High German' change of consonants (eighth century) which has made the distinction between the speakers of *High German* (most Germans and Austrians) and those of *Low German* (Dutch, Flemish, Frisian, some German dialects in rural areas, and English). A word like English *better*, which substantially retains to-day the root-sounds it had among the Anglo-Saxons, became by the High German consonant-shift the German *besser*, the other Low German dialects agreeing with English. Old English or Anglo-Saxon, then, belongs to the Low German sub-division of the Germanic group of languages and is derived from dialects spoken by the Germanic invaders of Romanized Britain.

The term Anglo-Saxon was never used of the language till the late seventeenth century, and even then only in its Latin form, since the first grammars were written in Latin. But as a name for the Germanic early inhabitants of England, writers of the ninth century using Latin had been known to use *Anglo-Saxones* to distinguish the English Saxons from their kinsmen who had remained on the German mainland. The term is also found at least once before the Norman Conquest in the vernacular. Bede has the expression *Angli sive Saxones* (Angles or Saxons), suggesting that Saxon had a wider implication than one tribe, and scholars, both in English and Latin, continued to refer to the language as 'Saxon' till the eighteenth century. But King Alfred, who first interested himself in English culture, calls the general language of England *Englisc*, and its peoples, whether

Angles, Saxons or Jutes, *Engle* (Angles). The expression 'Old English' is found in a prose work of the earliest thirteenth century.

It will be seen, therefore, that 'Old English' has apparent advantages over 'Anglo-Saxon' as the name of the language, though the latter is historically partly justified as the name of the peoples. This case is strengthened if we wish to think of the whole history of the language as a continuity: it is usual to speak of *Old English* (from the earliest writings till about 1100), *Middle English* (from about 1100 till the end of the Middle Ages), and *Modern English* from then onwards. On the other hand, as will be seen later, the dialect in which nearly all the important literature of the Anglo-Saxons is written is largely that of the South-South-West: whereas Modern literary English is much more derived from a midland type belonging to the East of the country mixed with a good deal of earlier South-Eastern. The idea of a clear continuity, therefore, in our literary monuments, as regards dialect, which the term Old English suggests, is somewhat illusory. The term Anglo-Saxon, besides having a considerable tradition behind it since the eighteenth century, may be thought to have the advantage of squarely facing the fact that the language of King Alfred is not the direct, but only the indirect ancestor of the English of to-day as it is written and spoken among the educated. But there is nothing to be said for the growing habit among journalists and political writers of using the term Anglo-Saxon as if it were the same as 'English-speaking'. It should be confined to the Germanic inhabitants of Britain before the Norman Conquest and to their language.

English, beginning with Anglo-Saxon or Old English, has developed many qualities of sound and syntax which differentiate it both from the original Common Germanic and from all the other Germanic tongues, and naturally Old English is distinguished by a number of special sound-changes which separate it in varying degrees from the other related Low German languages. But since our main object is to present a picture only in broad outline and to emphasize in little space only those aspects of English which have contributed permanently to the building of its special character, the details of Old English *phonology* (that is its sound-system) must be passed over here.

6. LANDMARKS IN THE HISTORY OF ENGLISH

Language is a natural human growth, partly mental and partly physical. It follows, therefore, that it never ceases to change, but is a continuing development in a constant state of flux. To divide the history of any language into 'periods' historically must, then, be only a somewhat artificial rough-and-ready expedient. Yet, provided it is remembered that such divisions are only approximate, the method has its advantages and is generally followed. The history of English is divided into three main periods, each of which may be further subdivided. They are *Old English*, *Middle English* and *Modern English* (this last is sometimes called *New English* after the example of German scholars).

The Old English period extends from the earliest written documents, about the close of the seventh century, to about 1100, by which time the effects of the Norman Conquest begin to be perceptible in the language. It is characterized by a homogeneous Anglo-Saxon language, with only a small amount of Latin influence, followed by some from Norse, on the vocabulary of the written language. It is also characterized by having its inflexional system relatively full, with three or four case-endings for its nouns and adjectives and fuller verbal endings than existed at any time later. In pronunciation it had no 'silent syllables' and its spelling was a rough attempt at being phonetic, that is to say its letters represented its sounds fairly closely. Its word-order was relatively free, since its inflexions prevented ambiguity. It had a number of dialects, but only one of them, the language of King Alfred's Wessex (West-Saxon), has left literary monuments on any large scale. For the history of the country caused this West-Saxon to become by the tenth century the accepted language for most vernacular literary purposes. Even the literature of other dialects, such as was most of the poetry, was re-copied into the 'standard' West-Saxon which, with local modifications, had become a sort of common literary language all over the country. It is this West-Saxon which, because there are most materials in it, has become the basis of Old English grammars and dictionaries. But, as has been already remarked, it is unfortunate that there is not a direct continuity between this literary West-Saxon and later English, since the direct ancestor of modern literary English was some kind of Midland (*Mercian* as it is called for the Old English period), with an underlay of South-Eastern. The nearest direct descendants of West-Saxon are to be found in such counties as Gloucester, Somerset and Devon, as rural speech only.

Middle English extends from about A.D. 1100 to about 1450, and may be said to take in the mediaeval period more narrowly so called. It begins with the Norman Conquest and ends with a transitional period leading to the close of the Middle Ages. It is marked by the sweeping changes in vocabulary caused first by the Scandinavian invasions and then by the Norman Conquest. For though the Norse invasions must have caused a general Scandinavianizing of the dialects in which they most operated, yet since the language of Northumbria and East Anglia and other lesser areas where Norsemen settled was scarcely written down in Old English times, it is only in Middle English documents that the real force of the Norse influence on the language becomes perceptible. The effects of the Norman Conquest and of the consequent French cultural influences later, were to deprive English finally of its homogeneous character. Norse, being fairly closely related to Old English, has left far less distinctive traces on the main stream of English than Norman French, which was not a Germanic language and had naturally far more 'foreign' ways with it. Inflexions, which had begun to weaken or become blurred in later Old English owing to the fixed stress already touched on (and perhaps helped by the mixing with the related Norse dialects of the earlier invaders), became definitely reduced in the Middle English period: and it is for this reason that it has been called the period of 'levelled' inflexions. This weakening of inflexions caused the word-order to become less free, as well as encouraging the growth of the use of prepositions and periphrases. Owing to the difficulties of the French scribes who became the chief copyists for a time in the twelfth and thirteenth centuries with the unfamiliar Old English spelling and some Anglo-Saxon letters not used on the Continent, there was in Middle English—especially in its earlier period—confusion in spelling and a loss of that phonetic habit with which Old English had begun. Some of the English letters had ceased adequately to represent a changing pronunciation in later Old English, and French scribes introduced some of their own Continental methods of spelling, so that uncertainty in orthography resulted. This confused spelling was further aggravated by the loss in the Middle English period of that idea of a kind of standard or common literary dialect which had been a feature of later Old English. The use of Latin for learned work, and of Norman French for aristocratic entertainment, reduced the English vernacular to a set of spoken dialects with little common impetus towards a norm or standard, and West-Saxon had no successor as a common literary vehicle. But this diversity of dialects for literary purposes remained even when, in the fourteenth century, the vernacular once again began to assert itself effectively as the language of English culture. It was only with the growth of London as the centre of commercial, political, legal and ecclesiastical life towards the end of this century that there began to emerge the dialect of educated Londoners as a widespread medium of written expression which was to become later the literary English we know. London's very heterogeneous population, drawn from all over the country, developed a kind of mixed dialect of the educated and commercial classes distinct from the local tongue of the streets whose modern direct descendant is 'Cockney'. The comparative nearness of the universities of Oxford and Cambridge (the only two in the country), with their similarly very mixed educated 'foreign' population, helped further to develop this new dialect of which London was the centre into something wider and more influential. But the East Anglian trade, especially that in wool and cloth, caused London to have particularly close connexions with the East Midlands; and it is for this reason that the educated heterogeneous population of London developed a very mixed dialect, spreading out to take in educated Oxford and Cambridge, which became largely East Midland in character while retaining an underlayer of the original South-Eastern of its geographical position. It will now be seen why it is that 'received standard' English is described as descending from an East Midland type of dialect rather than from King Alfred's West-Saxon. It was in the later Middle English period, then, that England's capital, as has happened in most countries, began to provide the whole country with its written language, though it was not till the late sixteenth century that this process may be said to have been completed, and not till two centuries later still that the same result was also achieved for the spoken language. This period ends with the introduction of printing to England by Caxton; and it is because so many rapid changes were going on in the language about that time as well as a corresponding transition from the Middle Ages to modern times in history generally, that it is convenient to regard the period from 1450 to about 1500 as one of transition from Middle to Modern English. This and the immediately preceding century were marked by a widening of the English vocabulary through technical Latin terms as well as through contacts with Continental European science and culture.

Modern (or New) English runs from about 1500 (or say about the end of the reign of Henry VII) to the present day: but it is clearly necessary to subdivide it at about 1700 (say Queen Anne's accession) into Early and Later Modern English. For though there are common factors which make the term suitable for the whole period, the language has changed so greatly between Henry VIII's time and now, that without such subdivision the expression 'Modern' for sixteenth-century works, for instance, is likely to sound forced or misleading.

Modern English covers the period conveniently, historically from the close of the Middle Ages and the completion of the Renaissance to the present age, which has all the appearances of being one of transition to another not yet clear. The division into Early and Later is made at about the point where spelling becomes more or less fixed in substantially its present form, and also the end of a period of exceptionally marked changes in pronunciation. Indeed it may be said that 1700, when Dryden died, is about the date from which we may fairly begin to think of English as having assumed the form which we still use. It might, however, in view of the considerable changes which seem to be taking place in English to-day, be a good thing to separate current usage from what history tells us about the language, and to speak of the tongue of our own generation as 'Present-day' English.

This Modern period is distinguished by a vast and varied increase in the Latin elements through the Renaissance influences, as well as by the loss of many of those inflexions which had been 'levelled' in Middle English. It is often called the period of 'lost inflexions' for this latter reason. Further fixation of word-order follows inflexional loss, as well as increased developments in prepositional usages and periphrases. But Modern English stands out from its predecessors markedly for the almost complete transformation in the pronunciation of its vowels, which took place between the beginning of the transition-period (1450) and the close of Early Modern English (1700). Especially between the fifteenth and seventeenth centuries English vowels, which had had very roughly the sounds of Classical Latin, came to assume their present sounds, some of which are peculiar to our language. This relatively rapid change in the vowel-sounds happened to coincide with the increasing and inevitable tendency of the printers, with the popularizing of books about Queen Elizabeth's time, to look for accepted conventions of spelling. The consequence of this was that the printers who based their conventions on what had been common a little earlier, lagged markedly behind the actual pronunciation by the time they had arrived at something like a common practice (about Dryden's later period): so that a marked characteristic of English in modern times is that its spelling, while fixed, is largely based on a relation to pronunciation which historically belongs to Late Middle English and Early Modern English; and pronunciation has changed considerably without being at all phonetically reflected in the orthography A notable feature of English, therefore, is now that its spelling is largely symbolical of thoughts and things rather than a phonetic representation of the actual sounds of the words.

7. PHILOLOGY AND LITERATURE

The term *Philology* originally meant, as used by classical and mediaeval writers, the study of literature, including the technical study of such linguistic matters as were needed for the understanding of texts. For the word properly means 'love of *Logos*': and *logos*, as has already been pointed out, implied both thought and language. To-day in England, though not in Europe generally, 'philology' has been narrowed till it covers only the more technical study of language apart from literature. Yet this distinction between 'language' and 'literature' in the approach to English, is clearly artificial as well as quite misleading and harmful. For there is no separating the two disciplines or studies. Only by understanding the meaning of an author's language, with the historical knowledge that this will imply for older literature, can any full aesthetic satisfaction be obtained. Without knowing something of the history of the language and of the meanings words and idioms have had at different periods of our literature, it will be impossible to appreciate Shakespeare, Milton or Pope; not to mention more obvious earlier examples such as Chaucer. It is, on the other hand, only in its written monuments that we can study the development of the English language: we must cultivate a feeling for the imaginative qualities in the use of words and a sensitiveness to their finer nuances of connotation, especially in poetry, if we are to know genuinely and intimately our mother tongue as employed by its best writers and speakers. The study of what is termed *Semantics* or *Semasiology*, that is of the meanings of words, is of particular importance to

the student of literature. So many words have
retained something like the same recognizable form
throughout their history, while the meaning has
continued to change through different periods. When
William Morris rendered a line of the Old English
poem *Beowulf* as

'The foamy-necked floater, most like to a *fowl*,'

he caused a somewhat comic and incongruous image
to appear in frivolous minds, because the word *fowl*,
which formerly meant any kind of bird, has long been
limited in ordinary usage to a particular species. We
must beware of thinking of the language as static
—assuming unconsciously that a word in Shakespeare
which is still in common use, must have had our
present significance to him. The famous line in
Hamlet describing King Hamlet as

'Unhousel'd, disappointed, unaneal'd,'

has the terms *unhousel'd* (from Old English *hūsel* =
'Sacrifice') meaning 'not having had the housel or
last Sacrament', *disappointed* in the sense of 'without
the proper appointments or rites of the Church', and
unaneal'd meaning 'lacking the Sacrament of anoint-
ing (*anealing*) or Extreme Unction'. All this is clear
to the student of the history of the language. But a
teacher is said once to have explained the line as
referring to the restlessness of the ghost lacking his
housel or 'little house' (coffin), while another is
alleged to have regarded *housel* as referring to the
bread of the Sacrament as a 'little house'. Clearly
either view would lead to distortion of the meaning
of the whole line and its context in the play, and
hence to a false view of Shakespeare.

But enough has been said to emphasize that one of the values of the study of the history of a language is that it constantly reminds the student that language is by its nature fluid, never static, a living organism which can only be fully appreciated in relation to thought and feeling as well as form.

CHAPTER II

VOCABULARY

I. GENERAL REMARKS

OF ALL world-languages English probably has the vocabulary which is the most copious, heterogeneous and varied. In it, as it were, there lies fossilized or still showing the signs of the freshness of its assimilation, the whole of English history, external and internal, political and social. All the peoples with whom its speakers have come into contact during the more than thirteen centuries of its growth, whether these contacts have been deep and lasting like those of France and ancient Rome, or casual like those of Spain or Czechoslovakia, have almost without exception left permanent marks on the vocabulary. The Romans with whom the ancient Germanic tribes had dealings, the Romanized Britons, the Latin Fathers of the Church who were once so eagerly studied, the Danish and Norwegian invaders, the Norman French conquerors, the revived ancient Latin and Greek Classics at the Renaissance, the Italian artists and men of letters of the sixteenth century, the great colonizing nations of the same century—all these have made their contribution to the English vocabulary. Arab mathematicians from Spain have enriched our language, as have American redskins and Indian sepoys. Alike the 'Italianate Englishmen' of Queen Elizabeth's time of whom Shakespeare made fun, and the Frenchified fops of the Restoration satirized by Dryden, have left something of value in the English word-hoard. It is, no doubt, true that such statements might fairly be made about other languages and their history: but what stands out so remarkably about English is the abundance, the unparalleled variety and the length of time during which foreign influences have been effective in its vocabulary. Also, it may be said, no other language has so much retained its nucleus of native words in ordinary use and its native primary grammatical structure, while assimilating such copious and heterogeneous material.

This abundance of finely graded words has made English quite exceptionally rich in its powers of expression: but at the same time one must pay heed to Samuel Johnson's warning of the 'copious vagueness' of English. The more abundant and varied the vocabulary, the more difficult it must be to use it with exactness and clarity. For example, a largely Latinized vocabulary may be the source of great enrichment to the language of a man who is familiar with Latin: but to one who has never come into contact with Latin at all, this very richness becomes a source of looseness and vagueness of expression, or a cause of temptation by the lure of mere sounding phrases and meaningless grandiloquence. The full and effective use of the English vocabulary is now the prerogative of the really well educated: and it is clear that one of the dangers to clear speaking and thinking in a democratic age where education tends to become more and more widespread and therefore less deeply based, is that the great instrument of the English language may prove too difficult to be used properly or may be played upon in a loose and slovenly manner.

No doubt the relative simplicity of the structure of

modern English and its astonishing flexibility and adaptableness have contributed to the ease with which every sort of foreign word or phrase, ancient or modern, seems to find naturally and easily a place in its vocabulary. English is peculiarly rich in what are, not quite accurately, termed synonyms: for there seem to be so many words and phrases which mean very nearly the same thing. But on closer examination, when one knows the full connotation and gets, so to speak, the full *feeling* of a word, it will be found that there are no such things as synonyms in the language, and that there is always some slight shade of difference in meaning or feeling or suggestiveness, between one word or phrase and another of like significance. This wealth of approximate synonyms is again a source of strength or of weakness to the user of English, according to his education for its employment.

Broadly speaking, words of deep emotional content are likely to be those long handed down from native English origin, whereas those of foreign descent are of shallower feeling. Thus, for instance, *love*, *hate*, *longing*, which are all native words, have a far deeper content of feeling than words such as *amatory*, *odium* and *desire*—of which the first two come from Latin and the last from French. Yet such foreign words in origin do have their exact shades of meaning and do contribute to the expressiveness of English if properly used.

It may be debated whether it is better for a language to be mainly homogeneous like Russian, or abundantly heterogeneous like English. A language that can, as could Old English, build up new words for new ideas from its own elements so that even the most technical terms have the sound and feel of native words, will have the strength which comes from unity of impression and the advantage of being fully understood most widely among its users. Except for a relatively small number of highly educated people, a language like modern English, with its vast tracts of thought which can scarcely be expressed without the aid of a Latinized vocabulary, must for many hearers lack something of naturalness and clarity in many areas of thought outside the common things and experiences of life. The power of creating new words for new thoughts and things which Old English had, was lost through centuries of atrophy after the Norman Conquest: so that when Reginald Pecock, a fifteenth-century theologian, tried to restore this linguistic gift by using such words as *ungothroughsome* for 'impenetrable' or coined the term *not-to-be-thought-uponable*, his efforts appeared unnatural and silly. The vast flood of new words needed at the Renaissance for the new ideas which so rapidly and from so many sides came to England, could by then only find expression in the coining or adaptation of numbers of words from Latin and other foreign sources. Yet, on the other hand, for those who can use English with its full compass exactly to express thoughts and feelings, its copious heterogeneousness is a real enrichment by reason of the subtle shades of meaning which the inclusion and assimilation of so much foreign vocabulary has made possible.

It will now be convenient to sketch and illustrate the influences of foreign tongues that have gone to the making of the English vocabulary and have also in so doing helped to mould English thought and expression. The major languages, from this point of view, will be treated separately, and then those whose influence has been only slight will be grouped together very briefly.

2. THE INFLUENCES OF LATIN

Contact with the Roman empire during several centuries had introduced the Germanic tribes to a number of Latin words before the Angles, Saxons and Jutes invaded England; and some of these words they seem to have brought with them. These, as might have been expected, were mostly words pertaining to the kinds of things which the contact with Roman civilization would make familiar to the Germanic peoples: military, Governmental, and trading terms, or names of materials the use of which would be new to the 'Germani'. We can recognize them by the fact that they are common to all or most of the Germanic dialects and that they shew in each of the Germanic languages that they had passed through changes of sound in them known to have been very early. Such words are *street* (originally a straight *paved* and hence Roman road)—Old English *strǣt* from Latin *strata* (*via*)—Old English *cāsere* (the word did not survive into Modern English, but was reformed at the Renaissance under direct Latin influence) from Latin *Caesar*; *mill*, Old English *mylen* from Latin *molina*; *cheese*, Old English *cēse*, from Latin *caseus*.

But though there was very little cultural contact between the Germanic invaders and the Romanized Britons who used Latin, at least in the towns, the natural conservatism of place-names has preserved at least one Latin word into English direct from the days of Roman Britain. It is the word *castra* which became Old English *ceaster* or *cæster*, and survives in so many names of places ending in -*chester* or -*caster* or -*cester*. So many places in Roman Britain were the seats of military garrisons that they came to be known as 'so-and-so camp' (castra): and one of these, *Chester*, was for so long the garrison-town of a particular Roman legion that it came to be called *legionis castra* 'the Legion's camp', and passed direct into Old English as *Legaceaster*. Other cultural contacts are perhaps suggested by such Old English words as *gigant* (Latin *gigantem*) 'giant' and Old English *orc* (Latin *orcus*) 'the lower world or Hades'. Barbarians were included in Roman armies in the days of the later Roman empire, and we may imagine the possible exchange of terms of folk-lore and mythology between Romans and 'Germani' over camp-fires, though this would be sheer guesswork.

The coming of Christian culture to England in a Latin form with the Roman missionaries and those from Ireland in the seventh century brought a few more Latin words, of which some have remained permanently part of the English language. Foreign ideas such as those of monastic living, bishops and priests, Christian symbolism, etc., had no native equivalents, except words already having heathen, and therefore undesirable, associations. So that a number of Latin words gave English terms that have remained with us. Such are *minster* (Old English *mynster*) from Latin *monasterium*; *monk* (Old English *munuc*) from Latin *monachus*; *bishop* (Old English *biscop*) from Latin *episcopus*; *priest* (Old English *prēost*) from Latin *presbyter*; *Mass* (Old English *mæsse*, from Latin *Missa*; *church* (Old English *cyrice*) from Latin *cyriacum*, etc. We need not concern ourselves with the fact that most of these Latin words were originally Greek, since it was only from their Latin forms that Old English adopted them. Nor need we pause over the difficulty of separating words of this Christian Latin source which may have come into other Germanic languages at the same time, from those which came direct into English.

It is interesting, however, to notice that, beside these Christian Latin words in early Old English times, there came into the language some permanent Christian words to express the new ideas also from purely native sources, or rather it would be more accurate to say that new meanings were given to existing heathen native words to express new Christian connotations. The Anglo-Saxons, for instance, before the missionaries arrived, had a great spring festival of revival which also began their year, celebrating their goddess of dawn *Eastru*: it was called *Ēastron*, which remains in the language as *Easter*. For when the Christians came with their great festival of the Resurrection (called in Latin *Pascha*), it seemed so like the native *Ēastron* that this word remained with an entirely new significance. Similarly, the Old English word *bletsian* 'to sprinkle with blood' has remained as *bless* owing to Latin Christian influence. For the heathen Old English priest sprinkled the blood of a sacrificed bull on the worshippers in order to communicate some magical power or strength to them: and when the Roman Christian priest gave his benediction in making the sign of the Cross, he too was communicating a divine favour to the worshippers: so that *bletsian* 'bless with

the sign of the Cross', came exactly to translate the
Latin *benedicere*. These odd examples are, of course,
exceptions to the general rule that words belonging
to the pagan religion should be replaced by others.

The largest number of Latin words, however, in
Old English belong, not to the direct influence of
Latin Christianity, but rather to the Latin learning
and science which came to England, especially in the
later tenth century through the great revitalizing of
Church life (and therefore of literature and science)
by the Benedictine revival which came across from
the Continent to produce such men as St. Dunstan
and the remarkable prose-writer Ælfric. Scientific
manuals like that of Byrhtferth, works on medicine
like the great collections of herbal recipes and
'charms' collected in the monasteries, and sermons
and treatises on theology and philosophy like those
of Ælfric, illustrate a new and much wider kind of
Latin influence, though little of it had any lasting
results for the language. Very many names of herbs
and trees, for example, in this way came into English
along with a number of technical terms. But though
relatively numerous, few of these have lasted: so that
from the point of view of the permanent building-up
of the English language, of the roughly four hundred
Latin words that at one time or another are recorded
in Old English, only about a score are in quite ordinary use to-day: and these are mostly of the earlier
Common Germanic or early Christian kinds.

But it was not only in the direct 'borrowing' of
Latin words into the vernacular that English was
enriched during this period. It had the power of
making new words from native elements, as has been
said: and in the later Old English period especially

this was notably exercised in the form of coining the equivalents of technical Latin words by means of a literal translation of the elements of Latin compounds into the corresponding English elements. Thus, to take an early example, the Latin (originally Greek) *Euangelium* is compounded of two Greek words *eu* 'well' and *angelion* 'news': and the Old English word *Gōdspell* is made merely by rendering these two elements into a corresponding Old English new compound. This *Gōdspell* is the original of our *Gospel*. Later this method of translating literally the Latin terms by specially coined new compounds, became a principal instrument in the hands of learned literary men for rendering their native language able to express the ideas of science and theology without recourse to Latin directly and without the assumption of any knowledge of Latin in their readers. Thus, Latin *Trinitatem* gives the new Old English word *þrynes* (literally 'the quality of being three'). Any child might soon understand this word as a religious term; whereas the modern *Trinity* by which later French-Latin influence replaced this word, requires considerable explanation since it contains no native English elements. Not only did Ælfric explain theology and philosophy and science by this method of making new English compounds from native elements to render Latin technical terms, but he even wrote a Latin grammar in the vernacular, in which the terms of grammar, such as names of parts of speech, were expressed by newly made native English words, such as *dǽl-nimend* ('part taker') for *participle*, *nama* for *noun* (Latin *nomen*) and *forsetennys* ('before-placing') for *preposition* (Latin *prae* 'before' and *positionem* 'placing'). Yet when in the nineteenth century

the Dorset philologist and poet William Barnes tried
to make modern English words of this type in his
English grammar, which he entitled *Speech-craft of
the English Tongue*, the results were merely regarded—
and rightly so—as eccentric oddities. For English had
lost this power of self-creation in the centuries following the Norman Conquest. Had not the French and
Latin influences come with the consequences of the
Norman invasion, English might well have developed
further this homogeneous power of self-creation: for
in the hands of Ælfric it was becoming a fit vehicle
for the expression of scientific and philosophic truth
through growth from its own resources.

Inevitably in such a historical sketch as the foregoing, only the written language can serve as direct
evidence. But we shall ignore the considerable
amount of later Latin influence on Old English
because it consisted mostly in terms which have left
no permanent mark on the language; whereas the
common words that the Anglo-Saxons brought with
them from Latin sources or received through the
influence of Christian Latin culture, must have been
part of the spoken as well as of the written language,
since they still remain in men's speech.

In the Middle English period it is much harder to
speak definitely of the Latin influence on the English
vocabulary, since French became the dominating
cultural and technical source for new words, and
French is only one of the developments in mediaeval
times of Latin. For one can scarcely distinguish
between words taken into English from French (of
which the ultimate indirect source must have been
Latin) from those adapted direct from Latin through
mediaeval learning and science. Only by carefully

looking at all the earliest forms can one come at a clear view on this matter for a particular word: and even then the early records are not likely to be anything like complete or consistently spelt. But besides these doubtful words from Latin, there appeared in increasing quantities throughout the Middle English period a number of purely technical legal, scientific and ecclesiastical terms taken direct from that language; and some of these have passed into far wider use and remained permanent parts of English. Such words are *pauper, proviso, equivalent* and *legitimate* (from the law), *index, scribe, simile* and *memento* (from science and the Schools), and *requiem, collect,* (noun), *diocese* and *mediator* (all from the Church). The vogue of translations from Latin in the fifteenth century greatly added to the number of direct Latin borrowings; and the common word *tolerance* first appears direct from Latin at this time.

By the beginning of the Middle English period English was still, despite its intake of foreign words, quite clearly a 'pure' or homogeneous language: but the progress of this period saw its passing definitely to the 'mixed' or heterogeneous state, though it was French rather than Latin which mainly brought this about.

It is, however, the Modern English period, from Henry VIII's reign onwards, that witnessed the main direct influences from Latin; and these were naturally especially strong and rapidly-working at the time of the Renaissance.

As the language primarily of the sources of European culture, Latin has been an influence upon English throughout its history, but with many fluctuations. The Renaissance brought the turning of the best minds directly to the ancient civilizations of Greece and Rome, and hence a direct influence from Classical Latin as distinct from the Latin of the Middle Ages. This mediaeval Latin was always a living language, since both the Church employed it for her services, and philosophers and scientists wrote naturally in it: but it had not the vitalizing force in its later stages of a new discovery such as was the 're-birth' in Western Europe of the ancient Classical language. But not only did a stream of Latin words and affixes enter English at this time: there was also a re-modelling of the schools so that men chosen for education or able to obtain it now went to schools in which the instruction was in Latin and the chief subject of study the ancient Classical languages and literature. Consequently, in Queen Elizabeth's time it was quite natural for educated men to use Latin terms or affixes unconsciously in their ordinary English speech. Shakespeare has been regarded as the inventor of the terms *castigate*, *auspicious* and *critic* because they appear to have been first recorded in his plays. But our records are often fortuitous, and never complete: and it is likely that anyone among Shakespeare's contemporaries of the more educated sort would have used these Latin words in conversation quite naturally and unconsciously. Their first appearance in Shakespeare is probably only an accident of little significance for him. We are too apt to think of Latin in the sixteenth and seventeenth centuries as the remote and foreign-seeming thing it is to most of us, even among the educated, to-day. In the sixteenth century, at least when the master was within hearing, boys in grammar schools talked in Latin as well as studied it: and when, as a result of the vitalizing impulses of the Renaissance, scholars began to turn their minds to their own vernaculars and how they might be made to emulate the good qualities of Latin, it was natural that the first English grammars should be written either in Latin or under the direct influence of Latin standards.

Besides the vast influence of Latin as the source of new words for new ideas at the time of the Renaissance when such a flood of new thoughts and knowledge came to England, the whole attitude to the language of its teachers and improvers in England was profoundly and permanently influenced by ideas acquired through a primarily Classical education and Latin grammatical models. A glance at any but the most recent grammar-book will remind the reader how the whole set-up and terminology of English grammar has been dominated by Latinate schoolmasters. Though Latin is no longer seriously taught in the majority of English schools, its standards and grammatical terminology continue still to some extent to dominate the formal study of the language. English is a Germanic language, belonging therefore to a different group of the Indo-European family from Latin: yet the ghost of the Latinate tradition still haunts our classes. For instance, though it has long been natural and proper to say colloquially 'it's me' or 'It was her', there are many teachers and other seekers after 'correctness' in speech who would insist on putting these supposed solecisms right to 'It is I' and 'It was she', on the ground that *me* and *her* are properly accusative or objective cases and that the verb *to be* must always take the nominative. Yet 'good English' must always be the usage of good speakers or writers, whether the Latin tradition agrees with this or not. Similarly, the common mis-use of *whom* for *who* by journalists and others is largely due to this Latinate tradition still influencing people who no longer have any real contact with Latin grammar. Again in metre we see the influence of an artificial Latin tradition. For English metre is based on stress or emphasis, not on quantity or length of syllable: yet teachers and text-books of metre still speak of *iambs* and *trochees* and *dactyls*; terms based on quantitive notions of syllables taken from Latin prosody and not at any time appropriate to English tradition or usage. Milton, in the Preface to his *Paradise Lost*, speaks of his own blank verse as observing 'fit quantity of syllable', though his real intention should have been on the appropriate arrangement of stress.

Scientific and philosophical works were normally written in Latin in the sixteenth to eighteenth centuries, and both Francis Bacon and Sir Isaac Newton wrote their great books in that language. It was natural, therefore, that the vast expansion of all kinds of science and philosophy which characterized the modern period should find the new words it needed in Latin adaptations into English. It is true that this practice received many kinds of opposition, and the indiscriminate use of Latinizing words has been made fun of by Shakespeare as well as by many Elizabethans. It is true too that the Royal Society, founded in 1662, had a special committee to try to improve the use of the vernacular for the writing of scientific papers: but its striving after what it called 'a close, naked, natural way of writing' did not stop the endless coining of new words for technical and scientific purposes. Indeed this practice continues to this day, though very few scientists have any real knowledge of the Latin from which their new coinages are meant to be drawn. A habit of borrowing whenever necessary from Latin (and from Greek through it) which was natural when men of science had a wide Classical education, has become in a sense quite artificial with the narrowing of the culture and Classical knowledge of such men which has taken place in more recent times. Worse still, much of the scientific terminology has passed with varying degrees of looseness of usage and misunderstanding, into the language of popular writers and speakers who are entirely without the sort of education that such a habit should imply.

On the other hand, the seventeenth century, for example, was really a learned age when it was natural for writers to use many Latinate terms: and a work of that period which seems to us to-day full of unnatural Latinisms may have been quite proper in its own time.

The language of Milton or of Sir Thomas Browne, which appears to us so full of 'un-English' Latin words, must have seemed far more natural English to men of the seventeenth century for whom those authors wrote. Their public was small but select, as well as having received an exacting Classical education in comparison with the vast numbers who to-day may read an author's works; and our reading public is, taken as a whole, almost entirely innocent of Latin. Moreover, many words of Latin origin that were current in the seventeenth century have not remained in use, and now seem merely bookish or pedantic.

Among the common Latin words which came into

the language in the modern period since 1500, the following, chosen from the respective centuries in order, may serve as typical.

Sixteenth century:—*exit, genius, area, fungus, miser, circus, vacuum, medium, species, ignoramus, vagary*.

Seventeenth century:—*torpor, specimen, arena, apparatus, focus, album, complex, minimum, status, lens, pendulum*.

Eighteenth century:—*nucleus, inertia, alibi, ultimatum, extra, insomnia, bonus* (noun), *via* (preposition), *deficit*.

Nineteenth century:—*opus, ego, moratorium, referendum, bacillus*.

These are Latin words which have been taken over unchanged: but the number that have been 'Englished' by taking on native endings or reductions is legion. Latin suffixes such as *-ate* (from *-atus*), *-ic* (from *-icus*) and *-al* (from *-alis*), for instance, have become part of the language, as in *educate, elastic* and *abysmal*. Sometimes too such suffixes are added to words that are of purely English origin, as in *fistic* as an adjective from *fist*.

This vast influence from Latin, however, though it has enriched the vocabulary so immensely, has not affected the natural structure of English very much, though its effect on literary style was considerable in the centuries when Cicero's prose was a natural model.

3. GREEK INFLUENCE

As has been indicated already, it is scarcely possible or profitable to separate Greek from Latin influence, because almost always it was through

Latin or in Latinized forms that Greek words came to English, Greek having been the culture from which so much of the content of Roman civilization was derived. As might be expected, too, nearly all Greek terms have come through learned, technical or scientific usage. Because of the comparative abundance of Greek scientific and philosophical terms, it has come about that certain large classes of technical words have continued to be made up from Greek, or latterly as often from elements of Greek put together by men with no real knowledge of that language. Moreover, certain Greek elements have become acclimatized in the English language for technical terms, such as *graph* (writing), *phone* (sound), etc. Thus such words for new inventions as *telephone* (*tele* 'far' and *phone* 'sound'), *phonograph* (sound-writing), etc.: and as an example of words coined without actual knowledge of the Classical elements, we may take *dictaphone* (in which the first part is Latin), or *appendicitis* (in which again the first portion is Latin and only the suffix Greek). Yet some of these Greek technical terms have become familiar to the multitude and come into common use (often with widened and loose meaning, such as *atom, character, chorus, cycle,* and *acrobat*).

Greek having been the European language which most fully and effectively developed the expression of philosophical ideas, it is natural that philosophical and related terms should, even though coming to English in Latin dress, have been founded upon Classical Greek originals. A *peripatetic* teacher (from Greek *peripatetikos* 'walking about') is still purely a technical term, though it appears occasionally in more popular writing. But *phenomenal* (an adjective made with Latin -*al* suffix from Greek *phainomenon* 'that which appears'), though properly a technical term in philosophy as in the expression 'the phenomenal world' meaning 'the world as it appears physically', has come in journalistic and popular language to be merely a synonym for 'extraordinary', so that we may hear of 'phenomenal weather', for instance.

Before the close of the Middle Ages, English had acquired from Greek, *academy, atom, Bible* (Greek *biblos* 'book'), *diphthong, harmony, ecstasy, nymph, tragedy, tyrant* and *theatre.* The sixteenth century provided *irony, alphabet, drama, elegy, dilemma* (a term from logic), *caustic, chorus, basis, pathos, larynx, epic* and *theory.* The next century gave *orchestra, pandemonium, museum, hyphen, dogma,* and *clinic*: while the eighteenth produced *bathos* and *philander.* The last century saw the coining or adaptation of *phase, pylon, acrobat, therm* and *agnostic.* Many of the foregoing came through Latin or French, and most are now part of what may be termed the *Common European* vocabulary.

Like Latin words in English, those from Greek are sometimes so far absorbed into the native complex as to be capable of new formations in English with English prefixes or suffixes; and similarly there are Greek prefixes and suffixes that may be attached to English words. Thus, just as we have *un*propitious (Latin *propitius*), human*eness* (Latin *humanus*) and concurrent*ly* (Latin *concurrentem*) where the Italicized elements are English, or *post*-war, and *infra*-red— in which the words are English with Latin prefixes, so too we have the Greek prefixes *anti* (against) and *hyper* (beyond) joined to English words in *anti*-British and *hyper*-sensitive; the Greek negative prefix *a*- is in *amoral*: and the Greek element *-ology* can be added to words of Latin English origin, as in *sociology* (Latin *socius*).

Medical science—partly through the great pioneering work and reputation of the Greek writers Hippocrates and Galen (from whom come so many of its technical terms)—has continued to take large numbers of words from Greek and to form new coinages on Greek (real or supposed) models. *Psychology* (from *psyché* 'mind') and *neurology* (from *neura* 'nerve') are fairly recent examples; and *hepatic* (Greek *hepata* 'liver') and *phlebotomy* (*phlebo-* 'vein' and *tomē* 'cutting') are old instances.

It is to be remembered that whereas Latin at the Renaissance was only the revitalizing and enlargement of an already well-used source for linguistic enrichment, Greek was very much a new impulse. The rediscovery of ancient Classical Greek brought a new way of looking at life to England with a wealth of new thought that meant a fresh field of language, at least for the literary and the learned. It brought, for example, a whole new set of ideas and terms for political science. When new and individualistic ideas came to England early in the sixteenth century with, among other things, the Reformation, this new outlook was often associated with the introduction of ancient Greek to our universities which happened at just about the same time: and this time too was one in which many new material improvements and comforts were brought to England from overseas which brought new foreign words. Now it happened that one sign of the Renaissance, as it seemed to conservative Englishmen then, was the introduction of the new Dutch way of making beer with hops (for hitherto it had been innocent of hops) and the new Dutch drink was known as *beer* as distinct from *ale* which was the traditional English drink. Not ineptly, then, did some nameless wag of Henry VIII's reign express the trends of his times in this couplet:

> 'Greek, heresy and beer
> Came to England in one year.'

4. FRENCH INFLUENCES ON THE VOCABULARY

With Latin, French is one of the great fundamental formative influences on the English vocabulary. Even before the Norman Conquest social and political, as well as ecclesiastical intercourse had begun among the ruling classes between those of England and Normandy: for the Saxon king Ethelred the Unready (978 to 1016) had married a Norman princess, and eventually his son St. Edward the Confessor (1042 to 1066) came to the throne. The result of these reigns was to some small extent the placing in important positions in England of Norman nobles accompanied by their retainers and servants: and these caused the introduction of a few French words pertaining to the new culture and way of life. Moreover, these Normans were of Scandinavian race, having come to France more than a century earlier and rapidly adopted Northern French as their language. They were, that is, of Germanic stock like the English whom they were soon to conquer. Before the Norman Conquest, we find, in English, French words of the kind one would thus expect, though only a few. *Castel* to mark the new type of fortified building in which the Norman noble was to live, replacing the

Old English word *burg*: *capun* (capon) suggesting the greater luxury of French cooking: and *bacun* (bacon) are examples.

With the Conquest and the re-ordering of the Government and upper social life of England which soon followed it, we begin to find, at first only gradually, but with increasing abundance as the twelfth century advances, the kind of French words which the influence of an 'occupying power' would suggest. A man is caught shooting a deer in the New Forest (a royal prerogative), and finds himself quickly surrounded by a group of armed jabbering foreigners who arrest him: and he quickly learns to recognize the new French term *prisun* (which is recorded in the reign of William the Conqueror): and terms like *foreste, tur* (tower), *market, rent, justise*, soon follow. After the Conquest, English remained the language of the country, but French of the Norman kind became that of the government and quickly became a necessity to many who had no share in ruling. The Church, the law-courts, the pleasures of the aristocracy, trade with the Continent, the art of war—all these and much else became Norman French in terminology. In the chronicle made by a monk of the monastery of Peterborough in about 1155 for the reign of King Stephen, though the writer is clearly an Englishman using his native idiom, we find such French terms as the following:—*acorden* (to come to agreement), *bataille, curt* (court), *cuntesse* (countess), *rent, tresor, carited* (charity), *pais* (peace), *miracle*, and *processiun*.

In the early thirteenth century, with the loss of Normandy and some other French possessions of the English by King John, the direct connexion between England and Normandy was weakened: and as the

century advanced, the English and the Normans
tended more and more to become one people, though
it was not till the next century that English became
the accepted language for a large part of literature as
well as for speech among the upper classes. A charter
of Royal proclamation was first issued in both
English and French together in the year 1258; and
in little more than another hundred years Parliament
(whose name is another word of French origin)
decreed that its proceedings should be held in
English, though the law-courts continued to encourage the use of French in their very Frenchified
terminology and records for centuries longer. Indeed
we still may see how dominant French once was in
English law from the very large number of French
legal terms which remain in use, such as *lèse majesté*,
oyez (the imperative of French *ouïr* 'to hear' used
formally by heralds and criers), *plaintiff*, *defendant*,
privilege, *distraint*, *tort* (the French word for 'wrong'),
malfeasance, etc.

A new impulse was given to French influence early
in the thirteenth century, however, by the dominant
influence which France, with its then supreme university of Paris, came to exercise in matters of culture
and letters: and it was in this century that very many
cultural terms came into the language. But the
dialect of French which was becoming dominant
culturally in France by this time was that of the
Île-de-France from which Parisian was developed:
and this had certain marked differences in pronunciation from that of the Normans. The consequence
was that some Norman words already in English
were replaced by forms of the more Parisian French
type, or that words of this latter class came into the

language with different meanings from others of the same root which were already in English from Norman French. Thus, for instance, Norman French had a hard *c* (k) from Latin which the new French type replaced by *ch*: and the Norman French *w* corresponded to a French *g*. We may compare the older *canceler* with the later *chancellor*, *carited* (Latin *caritatem*) with *charity* (from French *charité*), *cattle* and *chattel* (with differentiation of meaning between the earlier and later French borrowings). *Wastel* (the Norman French term for a kind of fine bread) has no corresponding word to-day from later French; but we may compare with it the modern French *gâteau*. Cf. also *guardian* and *warden*, *guarantee* and *warrant*.

Naturally, with the centuries of French dominance in Church matters, many French terms of religious significance were taken into English, some of which have remained. Such are *miracle* already mentioned, *canun* (Canon), *capelein* (later replaced by French proper as *chaplain*), *Cardinal*, *Prior*, *Baptist*, *Seint* and *prophete*—all of which appear during the twelfth century. In the earlier Middle English period, which extends from about 1100 to 1300, when most of the commoner French words that have survived from early contacts came into English, the following examples may serve to shew something of the variety of borrowing (spellings as first recorded):—

Buildings: *castel*, *prisun*, *chapel*, and *tur*.

Religious: *Grace*, *merci*, *desputen* (dispute formally), *service*, *Passiun*, *miracle*, *religiun*, and *image*.

Military: *werre* (war, cf. modern French *guerre*), *bataille*.

Domestic: *basin*, *furneis* (furnace), *lamp*, *beast* (from Old French *beste*).

All these belong to the earlier Middle English period: but the fourteenth century saw a great increase in the number; and by this time many French words that had formerly been limited in use to the upper classes when they used English, had become integral parts of the English language. In the following famous passage from Chaucer, for example, all the words of French origin are Italicized. It is the opening of his Prologue to the *Canterbury Tales:*—

> Whan that *Aprill* with his shoures sote
> The droghte of *Marche* hath *perced* to the rote,
> And bathed every *veine* in swich *licour*
> Of which *vertu engendred* is the *flour,*
> Whan Zephirus eek with his swete breth
> *Inspired* hath in every holt and heth
> The *tendre* croppes, and the yonge sonne
> Hath in the Ram his halve *cours* yronne,
> And smale foules maken *melodye*
> That slepen al the nyght with open ye,
> (So priketh hem *Nature* in hir *corages,*)
> Than longen folk to goon on *pilgrimages*—
> And *palmers* for to seken *straunge* strondes
> To ferne halwes couth in sondry londes:
> And *specially* from every shires ende
> Of Engelond to Canterbury they wende,
> The holy blisful Martyr for to seke
> That hem hath holpen whan that they were seke.

In these eighteen lines, omitting proper names and the word *martyr* (which may have come direct from Latin and is recorded already in Old English), we find that no less than eighteen of the words are French: and Chaucer is writing in a conversational style in the language of the educated London of his time. In more technical passages, such as descriptions of hunting, cooking, tournaments, etc., the relative proportions of French words would be a very great deal higher at this time.

Sometimes the older English word has survived alongside of its French equivalent, always with some differentiation of meaning, as, for example, *hallow* (Old English *hālig*) as in 'All Hallows Church' beside *saint*; *Writ* as in 'Holy Writ' beside *Scripture*; *board* beside *table*. This practice, together with that of retaining Norman French forms beside later 'central' French importations with some change in shade of meaning, has helped to make English so extraordinarily rich in synonyms, or rather in pairs of words which look like synonyms at first sight, but prove on examination to shew more or less subtle differences in significance.

In the later Middle English period the contacts with French which produced effects on English continued through the Hundred Years' War. But, as in so many ways, Middle English, which was especially characterized by general and widespread French influences on the vocabulary, is clearly differentiated from Modern English by its treatment of French loans. For with the close of the Middle Ages there came a marked change in the kinds of influence that French continued to exert (like Latin it has never ceased to be the source of new words). This change is marked particularly by two things. First, whereas Middle English had been generally receptive of French words which often became integral parts of the language, after the beginning of the sixteenth century, French became much more the source of particular classes of words, many of which were restricted to the better educated in use or to users of special groups of technical terms. Thus, for example, the sixteenth-century borrowings from French consisted mainly of terms pertaining to war. A second characteristic of later French loan-words is that they enter the language in their modern French pronunciation, and that this is partly retained and seldom or never fully anglicized: older French words, on the other hand, have been so fully assimilated to the genius of the English language that they have followed its successive changes in pronunciation and stress. One may compare such older loans as *table*, *chair*, *court*, *peace*, and *lake*—all of which would never be thought of as of French origin without some guidance—with *connoisseur*, *amateur*, *chef*, *valet*, and *garage*. In the second group the words all shew varying degrees of 'Englishing' in pronunciation: yet all retain something from the French sounds which is more French than English. They have not been so fully assimilated into the language as the other group. Early French borrowings, again, have generally adopted the native English system of stress, as, for example, *honour*, *reason*, *virtue*, and *favour*. In these, too, it will be noticed that the sounds of the vowels as well as the stress has become completely English. But such words as *connoisseur*, *bagatelle*, *bizarre*, *façade*, and *ménage* tend to shew a stressed final syllable which is un-English.

The development of French in modern English shews well how vocabulary may indicate the history, especially the social history, of a nation: and in the following illustrations of French borrowings since 1500, this should be particularly borne in mind. Besides the military and naval terms which the history of the period might lead one to expect, we find trading and social words. The following are some sixteenth-century French words which have remained in common use; but it must be remembered that this period was not outstanding for French influence:—*pilot, sally, brigantine, rendez-vous* (originally a military term), *partisan, cache* (hiding-place), *corsair, volley, indigo* (through French from Spanish), *sou, vase, fricassée, moustache, promenade, piquant, machine.*

The seventeenth century was of more significance in the story of French influence on the English vocabulary, because it was a period of exceptionally close contacts between the two nations in matters of literature and social intercourse. A lady at Charles I's court was despised if she could not speak fashionable French. The returned exiles among the Cavaliers after the Restoration of the monarchy in 1660 brought much cultural baggage from France; and the plays of the period abound with satire of the indiscriminate imitation of all things French among the 'smart set' in London. Dryden, the most widely representative author and critic of the later seventeenth century, was an enthusiastic follower in his earlier life of French dramatic models; it was he who first used the French word *correct* (as an adjective): and he devoted a whole play, his *Mariage à la Mode*, to making fun of the Frenchified English women of the age. At the same time the borrowings of military technical terms and others of commerce, continued. Here is a select and fairly representative list:—*dragoon, stockade, parole, reprimand, parterre, ballet, burlesque, tableau, chagrin* (spelt first as *shagreen*), *champagne, coquette, double-entendre, liaison, contretemps, par excellence, métier, verve, cortège, démarche, en passant, naïve, rapport, décor, forte, muslin, soup, group, quart, penchant.*

The eighteenth century was again rich in French entrants into English of all kinds, with military terms still continuing, and the growing importance of French as the language of diplomacy also making its mark. At its close a few special words called forth by the French Revolution appear. The list can only be very selective and arbitrary, but as before it will be confined to words and phrases in fairly common use. *Émigré, guillotine, régime, corps, manœuvre, sortie, espionage, tricolor, depot, fusillade, salon, bureau, canteen, critique, coterie, nuance, cul-de-sac, belles-lettres, brochure, rouge, rissole, liqueur, brunette, picnic, etiquette, ennui, gauche, passé, police, hors-de-combat, poste restante, coup.*

The nineteenth century was the richest of all periods in French loans since Middle English times, especially in terms of art and letters, of textiles and furniture, with the usual borrowing of military words. A few examples are given below under some of the principal headings:—

Military: *barrage, communiqué, franc-tireur* (from the Franco-Prussian war of 1870), *chassis* (originally of a gun-carriage).

Furniture: *portière, chiffonier, reticule, parquet, bric-à-brac, cheval* glass.

Literature and art: *resumé, littérateur, cliché, rococo* (indirectly from Italian), *Renaissance, baton, matinée, motif, macabre, fin-de-siècle, première.*

Dress: *rosette, fichu, lorgnette, profile, crèpe, négligé, beret, suède, cretonne.*

Food: *restaurant, menu, chef, sauté, soufflé, mousse, fondant, gratin.*

Social: *raconteur, chauffeur, roué, habitué, élite, débutante, fiancée, distingué, chic, risqué, savoir faire.*

Diplomatic: *attaché, clientèle, prestige, impasse, chargé d'affaires, rapprochement, dossier, débâcle, raison d'être.*

In the twentieth century the process of borrowing from French has continued, aided by two world wars in which England and France were close allies. *Garage, revue, vers libre, fuselage, hangar, limousine,* and *camouflage.* This last was a military engineering term connected with mining in the later nineteenth century, but only acquired its present military meaning (together with a great widening in metaphorical use) in the twentieth century as a direct result of the war of 1914–18. There can be little doubt that the general process of taking in words from French, some permanently and others only temporarily, is still alive and likely to remain so. Generally one may recognize a recent entrant to English from French by its retention of most or all of its French pronunciation and stress: yet even a recent word like *garage*, because of its having spread to all classes, is rapidly passing into an almost entirely English pronunciation.

It will be noticed that among more recent borrowings from French there has been an increasing tendency to take in whole phrases, either as they stand in French, or by a literal translation. This habit first aroused the wrath of Dryden, then of Dr. Johnson: but it still continues. Thus we have *comme il faut, de trop, enfant terrible, amour propre*; as compared with translated French phrases such as *goes without saying* (va sans dire), *jumps to the eyes* (saute aux yeux), and *make a gaffe* (faire une gaffe). The language of journalism has even carried this fashion to the point of absurdity by inventing a 'French' expression *that gives one furiously to think*, of which the French original is not known. French phrases are good when addressed to a suitable reader or audience, provided the same thing cannot as effectively be expressed in English; but not otherwise as a rule.

5. SCANDINAVIAN ELEMENTS

The chief Norse influences on the English vocabulary belong properly to the history of the Old English period, though their effects only become visible in Middle English to any marked extent. This is because the Norse settlements were completed before the Norman Conquest, though the areas where most of these were situated did not produce records that have been preserved: and it was only in Middle English times that areas of strong Norse influence provided us with a written literature. In modern times there have only been casual and occasional borrowings from the Scandinavian tongues, as contacts have never been strong or continuous since the Middle Ages.

Yet the contribution of the so-called 'Viking' settlers has been a very vital factor in the growth of British civilization, and the permanent effects on the English language, though not very wide, have been deep. The facts about the word *Viking* may here be of interest. It was a Common Germanic word which appeared in Old English even before any Norse invasions could have taken place. The Old English form of it was *wīcing* (from *wīc* 'a settlement' and the termination *-ing* meaning something like 'pertaining to'), and the earliest sense, found in the early eighth century, was 'robber' or 'pirate': for settlements in those times were commonly brought about by force, and to the inhabitants displaced by them the new settlers seemed much like robbers. But the Common Germanic word developed a more precise sense in Scandinavia, as Old Norse *viking*, one who crossed the seas from Norway, whether for plunder, service under foreign kings, or the founding of new settlements or even for trade. Under the influence of the narrower meaning of the Old Norse *viking* in the tenth century, the Old English *wicing* came to be used as a name for the Norse invaders generally. But *wicing* did not survive the Middle Ages; and the modern *viking* in English is due to the interest in Scandinavian ancient literature at the time of the mediaeval revival in the England of the late eighteenth century. At that time *viking*, in its Old Norse form with a long vowel, was taken into English in its present sense. Modern Norse languages have changed the word to *viking* with a short vowel: but the *English* form is derived not from this, but from the older type. That is why *Viking* should be pronounced with a long vowel in English, as in accordance with tradition, as against modern Norse *Viking* with short vowel, which is used by some historians out of mistaken deference to present Scandinavian usage.

After sporadic raids and invasions for half a century, Norsemen or Vikings made permanent settlements in England from the year 850, first in East Anglia and later in the Northern counties. In the next century and a half further settlements were made in parts of the West Midlands including Southern Lancashire. During the tenth century, therefore, we may fairly imagine considerable tracts in these areas inhabited by speakers of Norse dialects: and these were in the next century or so gradually absorbed into the surrounding English **types of** speech, in which, naturally however, they left considerable masses of Norse words and phrases, and even grammatical forms. It was in this way that the Scandinavian influence came to English.

Now Anglo-Saxons and Norsemen could almost understand one another as far as the better cultivated speakers were concerned; and the Icelandic poet Gunnlaug 'Serpent-tongue' was able to recite a poem of his own to the English king Ethelred the Unready at his court with great success. For the dialects of the invaders, whether Danes, Norwegians, Swedes or Icelanders, were members of the Germanic family; and though the forms of grammar were very different, much of the vocabulary was shared between Old English and Old Norse dialects, with differences of pronunciation. Moreover, among the aristocracy of England and Scandinavia there was a common Germanic heroic tradition and many commonly inherited cultural features which Christianity in England had not obliterated (Christianity did not reach the Norse lands till the eleventh century). Hence the influences of the Norse dialects were both wide and intimate, as is shewn by the permanent place in English of purely Scandinavian words that are primary grammatical elements in the language, such as the pronouns *they* (Old Norse þei-), *them* (Old Norse þeim) and *their* (Old Norse þeira). Middle English literature shews us dialects in the North, North-West, and East Midlands which abound in Norse words and phrases: but Modern English, which is a very mixed language made up of several dialect-elements, has not preserved so many of them: and London, from which it is mainly derived, was never a centre of Norse influence. Because the first invaders, in the year 787 as recorded in the *Anglo-Saxon Chronicle*, were Danes, and since the invaders, whichever area in Scandinavia they came from, all seemed to talk and look much in the same way, it naturally became the regular practice among the English to speak of all Norsemen as *Danes* (Old English *Dene*). That is why historians often somewhat misleadingly refer to all the invaders as if they had been only Danes. At first the Norsemen plundered, slew, and obliterated cultural monuments as they raided: but later, as most of them came more or less to accept Christianity (the Danish king Canute was a zealous Christian), the natural affinities between Saxons and Norsemen—of race, Germanic tradition and language—asserted themselves, and the blending of the languages became inevitable.

Not only is it true that the areas of greatest Norse influence in Old English times have left scarcely any literary monuments, but also it is the fact that the one dialect of Old English that became the vehicle of nearly all the literature, was relatively very little influenced by Scandinavian. For King Alfred prevented the Norse conquest of his kingdom of Wessex, and by his work ensured that its dialect was to become the basis of the common literary language. Apart therefore from some technical terms that have been preserved in other dialects, especially the Northern, we find very little sign of Norse entry into the Old English vocabulary.

The type of words borrowed was naturally that pertaining to the customs, the skills or the institutions of the Norsemen; and a few such terms have become permanently part of the English language, though many were too technical and ephemeral to last.

It is usual to cite the Old Norse forms as they occur in writing: but since Norse was not written till about the time of the Norman Conquest of England as the result of the Christianizing of the Northlands, it is better to think of pre-written or 'Primitive Norse' forms as the originals of Old English words. Before the Conquest the following small list includes all those words of Norse origin that have remained in common use in modern times:—*lagu* 'law' (from Old Norse **lagu*), *felaga* 'fellow' (*félagi* 'partner'), *wrang* 'wrong' (**wrang*), *ūtlaga* 'outlaw' (*útlagi*), *eggian* 'egg' or 'urge', literally 'put an edge on' (*eggja*), *hūsbonda* 'housedweller' later 'husband' (*hús-bondi*), *þrǽll* 'thrall' (*þrǽll*). All of these, in their early contexts, will be found to have been connected in some degree with law; and the less common *husting* 'meeting in a house' later 'hustings' (*hústing*) may be added for the sake of completeness.

But the bulk of the Norse words in English, though they must have come during the Old English period, only appear in writing in Middle English. In very early Middle English, besides the Norse pronouns *they*, *them* and *their* already mentioned, we find the earliest spellings of our *skin* (Old Norse *skinn*), *root* (*rót*), *snare* (*snara*), *hit* (*hitta*), *take* (*taka*), *crooked* (*krók-* 'crook'), and *ragged* (**raggu* 'a tuft') in which last the ending is English.

There is no need to go into the vast numbers of Norse words which came to some of our dialects and are recorded first in Middle English. Many of them survive to-day in such areas as Yorkshire (the word

Riding is a survival of the Norse division of the land and means 'third part' (*þriðing*), Cumberland (where the sheep are still counted in partly Norse forms of the numerals) and East Anglia. Other common Norse borrowings that appear first in Middle English records are *ill* (Old Norse *illa* adv.), *gape* (*gapa*), *skill* (*skil*), *wing* (**weng-* and **wing-*), *want* 'be lacking' (**wanta*), *ransack* (*rann-saka*), *ugly* (*ugga* 'to fear'), *bleak* (*bleik-* 'pale'), *cross* (*krus* 'fierce'), *same* (*sam-*), *bathe* (*baða*), *loan* (*lán*), *both* (*baðir*), *scot* in the phrase *scot free* (*skot* 'tax'), *sky*, (*ský* 'cloud') and *weak* (**weik-*).

Looking at all the foregoing Norse words and comparing those of Latin origin, one is struck, for the most part, with the completeness with which they have become one with the language and the way they have exactly the same kind of feeling and connotation as words of purely Anglo-Saxon origin. Indeed these Norse loans do not really lessen the 'homogeneousness' of the language: it is Latin, and to a less extent French, of the greater sources of linguistic borrowing, that do this for us.

Since the Middle Ages loan-words from Scandinavian languages have been only occasional, and mostly belong to that technical vocabulary for things primarily associated with Norse countries which is part of what has been called 'Common European'. Such words are *ski* (pronounced [ʃiː] according to the Norwegian dialect from which it reached English first, or anglicized to [skiː]), *saga* (through the early eighteenth-century revival of interest in Northern antiquities), *fiord* (Norwegian *fjord*, Old Norse *fjorð*), *troll*, *viking*, *skald* and *maelstrom*. But in the phrase 'run the *gauntlet*' we find what looks like a genuine

F

English phrase which in fact owes itself to Old Norse: for *gauntlet* here is a disguised form of Old Norse *gatlop* 'road-leaping' due to the influence by analogy of that other word *gauntlet* (glove) which is properly French. Among new minerals *tungsten* is a direct loan from Swedish (*tung* 'heavy' and *sten* 'stone').

6. OTHER GERMANIC LANGUAGES

The influence of German (that is to say the 'High German' used in Germany and Austria to-day) is negligible, and consists almost entirely of instances from the Common European of German technical terms. Such are *zeitgeist*, *shale* (German *schale*), *mangelwurzel*, (*mangold* 'beet' and *wurzel* 'root'), *wolfram* (the mineral), *Schottische* (*Schottische Tanz* 'Scottish dance'), *yodel* (*jodeln*) and *kindergarten*: but *plunder* (*plündern*), which came into English in the seventeenth century, is partly an exception to this statement. Yet Dutch, the other most important Germanic language, has had quite a considerable influence, though even the most influential of the other languages have been relatively superficial when compared with the three main formative influences of Latin, French and Scandinavian.

Dutch contacts with England—and with the Dutch may be placed the closely related language of the Flemings of Belgium—have been frequent and close; and this is also to some extent true of that other language spoken in Holland, Frisian. Dutch, Flemish and Frisian, are closely related languages of the 'Low German' branch of Germanic to which English also belongs. In early times Frisian was especially close to Old English in vocabulary and sound, and the resemblance has persisted somewhat. A popular rhyme current fifty years ago emphasizes this fact:—

> 'Good butter and good cheese
> Is good English and good Friese.'

As the only other Western power which was of mercantile importance as well as Christian, Friesland had friendly relations with King Alfred the Great and taught him some of his knowledge of ship-building. Edward III brought over Flemish weavers and merchants, and the Flemish wealthy traders of London were among the objects of the wrath of the peasants in their revolt of 1381. Dutch and Flemish artists sometimes worked in England and held influential positions in the sixteenth and seventeenth centuries, and in the latter century there was much employing of Dutch engineers for their special knowledge and experience in draining fens and flooded country. English and Dutch fishermen had constant occasions of meeting throughout the Middle Ages and in modern times. The Spanish attempts to suppress Protestantism in Holland and Belgium in the sixteenth century brought many English soldiers and adventurers to those countries. Naval rivalries and fights over their colonial empires were a marked feature of Anglo-Dutch relations in the seventeenth century. Trade, especially in woollen goods and cloth, has been particularly important between the eastern ports of England and Holland. In the nineteenth century the struggle in South Africa (where a dialect of Dutch had become the language of the influential classes) has been the most recent source of

Dutch influence on English; and the close and friendly ties provided by the world war of 1939–45 bid fair to encourage some continuance of productive linguistic relationship.

Already in the Middle English period we find the common words *skipper* (Middle Dutch *schipper*, pronounced [*szipper*]), *deck* (*dec*), *hoist* (*hijschen*), *buoy* (*boje*), *bulwark* (*bolwerk*) and *marline* (*marlijn*) all testifying to the importance of the Dutch on the sea which was so long to continue. *Loiter* (*leuteren*), *spool* (*spoele*), *groove* (*groeve*) and *hop* (plant) are due to other sorts of technical collaboration; the last-named reminding us of the fact that it was the Dutch who first put hops into beer and introduced the practice into England. *Luck* (*luc*) and *booze* (*bouse*) suggest the familiarity of ordinary Englishmen with Dutch visitors. *Splint* (*splente*) and *hobble* (*hobelen*) also belong to this period. In the sixteenth and seventeenth centuries Dutch and Flemish influence continues and increases, with terms of many kinds like *cambric* (Flemish place-name *Camerijk*, Cambrai where the cloth was originally made), *splice* (*splissen*), *freebooter* (*vribueter*), *dock* (*docke*), *swabber*, *minx* (*mensch*, adjective in Neut. used as noun for a woman disparaged), *brandy-wine* (*brande-wijn*), *sloop* (*sloep*), *decoy* and *coy* (*kooi* 'cage'), *furlough* (*verlof*), *snuff* (*snuffen* as verb), *drill* (*drillen* 'bore a hole'). *Manikin* (*manneken*), originally an artist's 'lay-figure', and *landscape* (*lantscap* and *landschap*) remind us of the influence of Low German painting in England after the Renaissance.

One thing that strikes one in looking at these Low German words that have come to English over so long a period, is that some of them seem to form a definitely colloquial or familiar class, to belong to 'low' or homely walks of life. Such are *booze* already mentioned, *dote* (*doten*) already found in Middle English *hanker* (*hankeren*) appearing first, in Elizabethan times, *hustle* (*hutselen*, with 'metathesis' or interchange of the *t* and the *s*), *boss* (*baas* from South Africa in the early nineteenth century), *dope* and *waggon* (*wagen*). Sometimes an originally technical term, such as *uproar* (*oproer* 'uprising' in military sense) has acquired a considerably different and wider meaning. Sometimes the Dutch word, like *manikin*, has become Common European and been re-introduced into recent English by way of French (cf. the more frequent English modern spelling *mannequin*). The well-used literary phrase *forlorn hope* was properly a military technical term (*verloren hoop*, meaning a specially picked troop for most dangerous work, literally 'lost troop', in which Dutch phrase *hoop* is the exact equivalent of the English *heap*). Both *forlorn hope* and *uproar*, whose sense has so far diverged from that of the original Dutch, belong to the Elizabethan period; but their military technical sense was soon forgotten with the passing of the Dutch wars, and the Dutch word *hoop* easily acquired the new meaning of 'hope' because it was pronounced roughly like it, just as the element *roer* of the Dutch *oproer* came to be associated with the English word *roar*. Of curious interest is the word *nitwit*, which preserves possibly the Dutch words *weet niet* 'I do not know'. It reminds us of the Low German workers who used to come to England in search of employment in times of persecution in their own country such as the early seventeenth century, when such men could only reply to their English questioners at first by repeating over and over in their own language *weet niet*—which may have caused them to be jocularly known as *nit-wits*. Such a Dutch apprentice is represented in Dekker's play *The Shoemaker's Holiday* in the early seventeenth century. But *nitwit* may more safely be derived from *nit* 'flee' and *wit* 'sense'; i.e. one who has no more sense than a flee: for the word is not found before the 20th century, though *nit* alone is already in Shakespeare.

Most of the terms from South African Dutch are of a purely technical local nature; but a few have passed into ordinary English. Such are *veldt*, *commandeer* (from the Boer War), *boer* (this had been used in the seventeenth century but only in the general sense of 'peasant'), and a few more. *Spook* (*spoek*) seems to have been borrowed through American English.

7. THE INFLUENCE OF ITALY

It is probable that numerically the Italian influence will seem greater than the Dutch, indeed the greatest after French, Latin and Scandinavian. But this counting of heads is misleading. For many Italian words only came to English by way of French, a very large number belong to the Common European vocabulary of technical terms, and most have retained an approximately Italian pronunciation and failed to reach those speakers of English who are outside of literary and artistic influence. For Italy, for obvious historical reasons, has been especially the source for terms of the arts—particularly music and painting; and the considerable influence of the Italian Renaissance on English literature, often exercised through France, has left a number of words belonging to literary criticism. But Italian influence, which is probably still operating, has nothing like the length of history of the linguistic contacts hitherto dealt with: for it only begins with the sixteenth century. Consequently, since no Italian words have been in the language for more than a very few centuries, they have not become intimate parts of the language as a rule. Only *pilgrim* (Italian *pelegrino*) may be cited as a possible example of Italian influence before the Tudor period: but this is not certain, as a French form like **pélegrin*, though not recorded, may have existed as the source in some dialect.

The Italians were impressed with the zest with which aristocratic Englishmen toured Italy in the sixteenth century and strove to be more Italian than the Italians. Hence the oft-quoted saying that 'An Italianate Englishman is a devil incarnate': and moralists and playwrights, including Shakespeare, frequently attacked the Italianate Englishman. But though there were hordes of temporary Italian entrants into English in Elizabethan times, only a few have remained in anything like wide use. Shakespeare refers to *stanza* as a new word, Spenser introduced *canto* to the language for the divisions of the books of his *Faerie Queene*, and the Elizabethan *madrigal* remains a fairly well-known term. *Pilaster, piazza, cupola, artichoke (articiocco), volcano, stiletto, broccoli, casino, arcade, dilettante, vendetta, spaghetti, Madonna, prima donna, replica, studio, seraglio, gondola* and *inferno*: all these are examples of Italian words that have a wider use than their original more technical purpose. The dominance of Italy in music and painting, which has produced in England, as in the rest of Europe, so many of the technical terms of those arts, needs no further illustration and cannot be said to have meant anything individual in the history of English.

8. OTHER EUROPEAN INFLUENCES

The influences from other European languages have in general only been very superficial, and have often been merely the sharing of some technical contribution to Common European. The most outstanding, and the only one of these influences upon the English vocabulary that has provided any considerable number of words permanently remaining in ordinary use, is Spanish. For contacts with Spain, one of the great powers in the sixteenth and seventeenth centuries and for long a dominant colonizing imperial power with vast American possessions, have been of some significance. These began with the marriage of Queen Mary to King Philip of Spain in the middle of the sixteenth century, and continued with wars and many competitive dealings in the Americas for the succeeding two hundred or so years. They have given English the following words still in common use, besides a good many more limited technical terms and a number of Common European words:—*renegade* (*renegado*), *grandee* (*grande* 'nobleman'), *spade* at cards (*spada* 'sword'), *cannibal* (*canibales*), *siesta, potato, mosquito, desperado, esplanade, stevedore* (*estivador*), *dago* (from the proper name *Diego*), *vamoose* in American English (from Spanish *vamos* 'let us go') and *canyon*.

With Portugal, despite the fact of a continuous alliance from the mid-fourteenth century, contacts have mostly been through the Portuguese colonial empire, especially in Asia and Africa. Perhaps *marmalade* is the best-known word of Portuguese origin (Portuguese *marmelada* 'quince jam', *marmelo* 'quince'); but even this, the earliest borrowing, before the end of the fifteenth century, was through the French. *Buffalo* (*búfalo*), *mandarin* (Portuguese *mandarin* taken through Malay), *caste* (*casta* 'race'), *pagoda*, and *ayah* (*aia*) are about the commonest examples: and of these only *caste* can be said to have abundant uses.

Celtic influences have been sporadic and almost negligible. For historical reasons there was practically no survival of British words among the Anglo-Saxons, though *brocc* 'badger', *torr* 'high rock', *cumb* 'valley' as in Devon and Somerset place-names (cf. Welsh *cwm*), may be examples. Yet only the last can be said to have in any way survived. In later times there have been borrowings from Welsh, Irish and Scottish Gaelic; but these have only been more or less limited and technical terms for the most part. *Druid*, which existed as *drȳ* in Old English, has been re-introduced from an Irish form, and *shamrock* (Irish *seamrog*), in the late sixteenth century; and in the eighteenth we have *banshee* (Irish *bean sidhe* 'fairy woman'). Later we find a number of merely Irish words for Irish things, such as *blarney* and *colleen*. But *brogue* (Irish *bróg*) and *galore* in colloquial speech (Irish *go leór* 'enough') are in wider use. Scottish Gaelic has supplied a number of words from the fourteenth century onwards, such as *clan* (Gaelic *clann*), *loch*, *bog* (*bogach*), *cairn*, *plaid*, *glen*, *whisky* (*uisge beatha* 'water of life'), and of course a number of specifically Scots technical words like *claymore*, *sporran* and *pibroch*. Wales has given English very little save a few technical terms for specifically Welsh conceptions like *eisteddfod*: but we may note *coracle* (Welsh *kwrwgyl*, remembering that Welsh pronounces *w* like long *u*), *bard*, *crag* (*craig*) and *kromlech*.

Cornish, which was a Celtic language spoken to some extent till the early eighteenth century, has left plenty of marks on local place-names and a few words in the present Cornish dialect of English: but it cannot be said to have had any significance for the development of the English vocabulary.

Of the Slavonic languages, Russian has given to English a few Common European terms, beginning with *sable* (Russian *sobol'* through French) in the fourteenth century, and these have considerably multiplied in the last thirty years or so owing to the very great importance of the new Soviet civilization. Apart from names of specifically Russian things like coins and measures, before the Bolshevik revolution of 1917 the most interesting word, and the nearest to ordinary usage also, is *mammoth*. This is from Russian *mamont*, misprinted without its *n* in the early eighteenth century at a time when *th* was still an occasional spelling for the sound of *t*. Thus in the first Russian grammar printed in England (at Oxford) by Ludolf, the Russian *mamont* appears as *mammoth*. A whole new set of connotations have developed in English as well as in the other European languages for such words as *Soviet* (originally 'Council'), *Bolshevik* (historically 'member of the majority') and in the native English word *red* because of the new connotations of its Russian equivalent (*krasny*). The only words from other Slavonic languages that are in fairly widespread use in English are the Common European *intelligentsia* (Russian from Polish) and *robot* (from Czech *robota* 'work') through the popularity of Karel Čapek's Czech play *Rossum's Universal Robots* which appeared in English dress in 1923.

Hungary will be found only to provide English with odd Common European terms such as *Magyar*, *goulash* and *paprika*: and similarly the other European countries have merely given English occasional special terms which are also part of the Common European technical vocabulary.

9. WORDS FROM OUTSIDE OF EUROPE

In view of the world-wide contacts of speakers of English—through competition with the empires of Spain, Portugal, the Netherlands and France, in Africa and the East, the Red-Indian languages by way of America, British dominion in India, Africa and the Far East, and the British settlement of the newly discovered continent of Australia in the eighteenth and early nineteenth centuries—it is not surprising that the English language has absorbed a various and heterogeneous quantity of words from almost everywhere, besides the natural growth of local technical terms in the different parts of the English-speaking world. But much of this is an indirect taking-over of Eastern or African words through other languages. A specially large group of local technical terms has grown up through the British rule in India, and a few of these have passed into the common language. But no systematic treatment of all this mixed material is possible here, especially as we are mainly only concerned with ordinary English as a whole and not with its many technical and local branches.

At first sight, however, it might seem that the Arabs deserve special consideration as an influence on English. For it was by way of the Arabs or Moors of

Spain and of Arabic-speaking great mediaeval centres of science and culture in the Middle East, that important technical terms came to English in the later Middle Ages. Through Spain and through contacts brought about by the Crusades, Islamic culture and the Arabic re-discovery of much of ancient Greek science and learning, served as an enlightening and revitalizing influence on Western European civilization. But on closer examination it will be found that almost all of the technical vocabulary brought from the Arabs—words like *algebra*, *cipher*, *zenith*, *saffron*, *admiral*, *cotton*, *amber*, *arsenal*, *assassin*, *magazine* in the sense of 'store', *alcohol* and *zero*—are merely part of the Common European vocabulary so often referred to. All such terms, also, seem to have come into English from other, usually Romance, languages. A much larger number of Arabic words denote things or ideas belonging properly to peoples of Arabic culture and are only used in English in connexion with such localized matters. Especially of this kind are most of the modern borrowings from Arabic, such as *fakir*, *imam*, *madrasah* ('school of Islamic study') and *harem* from the seventeenth century, *Allah*, *houri* ('gazelle-like woman of paradise'), and *hookah* from the eighteenth; and *yashmak* (nineteenth century). Of the Arabic words the following may be said to have gained wide use in non-technical ways in English: *ghoul* (Arabic *ghūl*) and the adjective *ghoulish* with English suffix, *syrop* (Arabic *sharāb*, but through French *sirop*), *cipher* (*çifr*, but through Spanish and French), *garble* (*gharbala* 'sift', but through Italian), *calibre* (*ǵalib* 'mould', through French), *magazine* (*makazin* 'store-house', through French and with transference of meaning), *alcove* (*al qobbah* 'the vault', through Spanish and French), *gazelle* (*ghazāl*, through French).

From India comes a nineteenth-century influence through the study of Sanskrit philosophy; and thus Sanskrit, which may be thought of as the classical language of Hindu India, has given English technical terms of religion, some of which have attained to a slightly wider use. *Nirvana* (Buddhist ultimate state of the good, literally '*blowing out*' of the candle) and *swastika* (symbol of good luck) are perhaps the most familiar: but *yoga* and *karma* have obtained some currency through imitators of some aspects of Hinduism. Besides the considerable 'Anglo-Indian' local vocabulary, from modern Indian dialects, among words that have a wider use in English, may be mentioned *sahib*, *nabob* (Hindi nāwāb); *mongoose* (Marathi, *māngŭs*); *dungaree*; *bungalow* (*banglā*); *juggernaut*, a special image of Vishnu, the Hindu god, (*jaggan nath*, 'Lord of the world'); *bangle*, (bangrī); *chit*, (chitthi); *shampoo*, (*champō*, imperative of *champna*, 'press'); *dinghy*, (*dengī*) and the colloquial *cushy*. This last seems to be derived from the Hindi (originally Persian) word, *khusi*, 'pleasure': and like a number of more ephemeral words from slang, came to England through soldiers returned from India.

Persian, which often has worked through Arabic, has contributed to the Common European vocabulary; and in English *azure*, *jasmin*, *lascar* and *khaki* through India, *shawl* (Persian *shāl*), and the terms of chess (the game may have originated in Persia), *rook* (*rūkh*) and *check* (*shah* 'king'). *Check-mate*, which belongs similarly to Common European, is ultimately from the two Persian words *shah māta* 'the king is dead'.

China has given English the common words *tea* (Amoy Chinese *t'e* through Dutch) which is Common European, and *kowtow* from the Chinese *k'o-t'ou*. *Kimono*, *hara-kiri*, *geisha* and *jujitsu* are the best known terms from Japan with a slightly wider than local use. *Boomerang* from the Australian bushmen; *orangoutang* (*ōrang ūtan* 'forest man') from Borneo; *bamboo*, *sago* and the adverb *amok* (Malay *amuk*) in the phrase 'to run amok' from Malaya; *squaw* from the American Redskins; *igloo* from the Eskimos; *chimpanzee* from Portuguese Africa; *canoe* and *potato* (through Spanish *patata*) from Haiti; *tattoo* (Polynesian *tatau*) from the South Sea Islands, and the Tongan word *taboo* (*tabu*). All these attest how varied and how far-flung have been the influences which have moulded the modern English vocabulary. All the above examples too are of words which have a real place in the language and are not merely technical or local.

10. RECENT AND CURRENT TENDENCIES

One difficulty in dealing with recent and current happenings in the language is that we are likely to find ourselves too near in time to the occurrences concerned, and too uncertain of their chances of survival or permanence, to be able to form a clear picture of them or to judge of their value. World-shaking events like the two world wars of 1914–18 and 1939–45 have left vivid marks upon both popular and literary language: but already some of these have begun to fade, while others look like remaining. *Camouflage*, which owes its currency to the war of 1914–18, has so many uses of a metaphorical kind that it does not seem likely to disappear. But one would hesitate to pronounce on the permanent value or prospects of *blitz* (from German *blitzkrieg* 'lightning war'), or *evacuee*. Or again, many Americanisms have come into the language as the result of all kinds of contacts with the United States of America, particularly the two recent world wars and the immense vogue of the cinema in which America has been so much a pioneer. *O.K.* (supposed to have arisen from an illiterate postman's use of the letters *O* and *K* for *orl krekt* 'all correct') bids fair to becoming established in the colloquial language. But *intermission* and the at present vulgar phrase *'you're telling me'* seem far less probable survivors.

Slang is the language of a particular class or occupational group which has passed at least to some extent into colloquial usage: the *cant* of the special class or group becomes slang when so extended: and sometimes this slang may become acceptable permanently even in the literary language. Thus, for instance, a certain Captain Boycott in the Ireland of the land-disputes of the 1880's was isolated by his tenants and could get no labour for his farms: and this kind of act became known locally as a *boycott*, and then a verb to *boycott* was developed in general use. This expression, first as cant and then as slang, has become an accepted part of the English language, as it has gained general currency among educated speakers in England. How much of the cant of the war of 1939–45 has become slang? And how much of such slang will become acceptable colloquial and literary English? It is clearly too soon to answer this question. Similarly, some of the cant of the film industry has passed into English slang: but this may be only ephemeral, or on the other hand some of it may be found so valuable as to last. Some American usages of English have already become part of the literary language, such as *sense* as a verb, *viewpoint*, or *filibuster*. But it seems unlikely that many of the colloquialisms from American 'low life' which the films make popular among the young people of to-day, will endure. Again, because American English is in large measure a development of English of the seventeenth and eighteenth centuries, it has preserved some good words and phrases which have become obsolete in the language of Britain. Such a word as *fall* 'autumn', reminding us as it does of Shakespeare's *'fall of leaf'*, may well return to its place in the best English usage.

The foregoing survey of the development of the English vocabulary, in which an ever-widening series of foreign influences has received the main attention, should not lead the reader to think that English has grown in wealth only through these additions. It is true that the language passed in the Middle English period from its earlier 'pure' state to one of mixture or heterogeneousness, and that the native power of self-creation in words was largely lost through atrophy. But this power never entirely ceased to exist; and especially during the Elizabethan period and in the nineteenth century, it partly was revived by the deliberate efforts of writers. Renaissance authors, conscious of the dangers of too sudden and rapid a recourse to Latin in indiscriminate borrowing for new ideas and things, revived a number of older words of native stock, especially for poetry, and invented new English compounds. Spenser, Shakespeare and the translators of the Authorized Version of the Bible in 1611 all illustrate this fact. In the nineteenth century there was another deliberate attempt to enrich and revitalize the language by seeking to replace some of the less attractive Latin words by developing the English words they had replaced. Thus, for instance, *manual* was replaced by *hand-book* which had been used by King Alfred in Old English as *handbōc*. The Dorset poet William Barnes, mentioned earlier for his *Speechcraft of the English Tongue*, seemed ridiculous with his new term *markword of suchness* for *adjective*. Yet his zeal for 'English English' had some healthful effects, though *folk-wain* failed to replace the Latin *omnibus* and its later abbreviation *bus*. William Morris, too, did much for the native elements in the language. In the twentieth century many new words are formed from English roots, often beside foreign-based equivalents. *Wireless* has become as common as *radio*, *wire* is more frequent colloquially than *telegram*, and there seems a possibility that *walker* may replace *pedestrian*. There is a reaction against the Latinate vocabulary loosely used, the circumlocutions and the stereotyped phrases of official and commercial language, in favour of simpler and more direct native forms of greater clarity. Indeed it may be said that the 'copious vagueness' in the common use of the English vocabulary continues side by side with a deliberate looking for the native clearness and simplicity that can only come from a vocabulary fully possessed by the user. Attempts, in view of English possibly becoming even more of a world-language than it is, at reducing and simplifying its vast vocabulary to a thousand or less words for the supposed benefit of foreigners, such as *Basic English*,

G

are, however, scarcely likely to lead to permanent
results: for language is an ever-changing and developing expression of human personality, and does not
grow well under rigorous direction.

Our account too illustrates how intimately British
history, especially social history, is linked to the
English vocabulary. Given a knowledge of the origin
of English words, we could in fact deduce most of the
history of England from the story of its vocabulary.

Another feature of recent English is the amazingly
rapid ramifying and expansion which have taken
place and continue to arise in the meaning of words
once of simple connotation. Consider, for example,
how the meaning of the word *labour* has multiplied a
hundred-fold in the last fifty years with the growth
of the 'Labour' movement and its political implica-
tions. Or again such terms as *democracy, socialism,
communism* and *fascism*. Any of these will be found
to have half a dozen different meanings and implica-
tions among any large and varied group of not very
well educated persons. Some words, perhaps, may
seem to be becoming overworked and rendered useless
almost by the vagaries and looseness of their mani-
fold uses.

Perhaps the best justification for the accurate study
of the English vocabulary in all its bearings will be
found to be the consciousness of the difficulties and of
the rewards for its users that such a study will
arouse. It was a Frenchman who said 'The style is
the man': but it was the Englishman Swift who
described a good style as, 'Proper words in proper
places'.

CHAPTER III

SPELLING AND PRONUNCIATION

I. GENERAL CONSIDERATIONS

ONE of the outstanding features of English is the apparent discrepancy between its spelling and its pronunciation. Throughout its history, English has had scribes, printers and conscious reformers who have tried to make spelling adequately represent pronunciation. But always the pronunciation has changed quicker than the spelling, and latterly in the modern period the conventions of printing have standardized the spelling, leaving pronunciation to continue its natural course of change. Before we can discuss this question effectively, it will be necessary to have at least a rough method of writing down sounds quite independent of the spelling they may have had at any given time in the history of the language. How often do writings of foreign words or of those of other dialects fail to indicate the appropriate noises to us because there is no agreed system by which every sound should have its fixed symbol in writing! The science of *phonetics* treats of the noises we make in speech quite independently of the manner of writing them in ordinary books. It has therefore found it necessary to invent such a 'phonetic' writing, by which the actual noises of any language or dialect can be written accurately without regard to conventions of spelling. Thus it is quite possible for a person with a trained ear to write down a foreign language as he hears it without any understanding of its meaning, and then to have his 'phonetic transcript' translated by those who do know the language. Or again, many unwritten languages, such as those of some American Indians, have been written down from mere hearing, so that their structure might later be reached and a suitable alphabet devised. It will be convenient then, to use when necessary in the following sketch, a simplified form of the phonetic writing authorized by the *International Phonetic Association*. It is as follows:

VOWELS

Phonetic symbol	*Current spelling*	*Phonetic transcription*
ɑ	*patte* (French)	pɑt
ɑː	*father*	fɑːðə
æ	*hat*	hæt
ɛ	*met*	mɛt
ɛː	*bête* (French)	bɛːt
e	*été* (French)	ete
i	*bit*	bit
iː	*machine*	məʃiːn
ɔ	*not*	nɔt
ɔː	*bought*	bɔːt
oː	*beau* (French)	boː
u	*foot*	fut
uː	*boot*	buːt
y	*but* (French)	by
yː	*lune* (French)	lyːn
ə	*china* (last syll.)	tʃaínə
ʌ	*but*	bʌt
ai	*bite*	bait
ei	*play*	plei
ɑu	*house*	hɑus
ou	*stone*	stoun
ŋ	*finger*	fiŋə

CONSONANTS

Phonetic symbol	Current spelling	Phonetic transcription
j	*your* (initial)	juːə
g	*good*	gud
k	*cat*	kæt
ð	*then*	ðɛn
þ	*thin*	þin
kw	*quick*	kwik
ʃ	*shin*	ʃin
tʃ	*chin*	tʃin
χ	*loch*	lɔχ
z	*zebra*	zɛbrə
s	*silk*	silk
ž	*measure*	mɛžə
dž	*jam*	džæm

The other consonants are pronounced much as in English to-day.

In using the above phonetic method, the following points are to be remembered:—

(*a*) The so-called 'liquids' *l, r,* and the 'nasal' consonants *m* and *n* may be also pronounced as syllables, when a mark may be placed beneath them. Thus in *table* [teibl̩], the *l* is syllabic, as compared with *tabloid* [tæblɔid]. Similarly compare the *m* in *prism* [prizm̩] with *prismatic* [prizmætik], the *n* in *nag* [næg] with that in *ration* [ræʃn̩], etc.

(*b*) All phonetic transcriptions are placed within square brackets to distinguish them from actual spellings.

(*c*) The syllable having the strong stress may be marked with an acute accent, as in *bacon* [béikn̩].

unintelligible in Britain, can communicate satisfactorily in the written form, since to them the groups of letters are the symbols of words and not of sounds. It is, on the one hand, the changing nature of pronunciation that makes the chief objection to any phonetic reform of English spelling, and on the other, the loss of continuity with the past and contact with older literature which would result from such a reform. 'Simplified spelling' or 'reformed spelling' is a far more complex and uncertain problem than those who have not studied the language scientifically can easily realize.

2. HISTORY OF SPELLING AND PRONUNCIATION

The Anglo-Saxon alphabet was an adaptation of the Roman letters by early Christian missionaries from Ireland so as to make it roughly a phonetic representation of the vernacular of their converts. It is by knowing the way these Irishmen must have pronounced their Latin and by comparing with other Germanic languages, that we are able to form some idea of how Old English was sounded. Sounds which did not exist in Latin were improvised by using letters from the heathen 'Runic' writing (which the Germanic peoples had among their priests and men of learning for magical and religious purposes and consisted mostly of straight-lined symbols scratched upon stone), or by inventing a new symbol. Thus we have, as has been said, the Old English sign þ from the Runic, and the ð invented newly by taking the Irish form of the Latin *d* and putting a line through its upper stroke. Both these letters represented *th*-sounds, and their functions were replaced by the *th* which we still use,

in the later Middle English period. But the early
printers and fifteenth-century scribes often used a *y*
in certain common words like *the* and *that* for this
symbol þ: and hence spellings such as *ye* for *the* and
yat for *that* are found as late as the eighteenth
century. *Ye* was a mere spelling and never had any
other pronunciation initially than our *th* [ð]: so that
the archaic phrase *ye Olde Englishe Ynne* should
not be thought to represent anything other than
the current pronunciation as regards the definite
article.

Whereas the consonants have changed relatively
not so markedly, English vowels, particularly the
long ones, have become almost completely trans-
formed during the history of the language. Up till
late in the Middle English period the changes were
not so great: but from the fifteenth to the seventeenth
centuries the long vowels and some of the short ones
moved very greatly in sound. If we take the year
1000, when Ælfric the great classical Old English
prose-writer flourished, as roughly typical for the Old
English period, Chaucer for the Middle English, and
Shakespeare for the Early Modern period, the table
on p. 92 may serve to indicate the main changes in
the pronunciation of the vowels that have taken
place during the history of English. Key-words are
placed in the left-hand column, the changes noted
chronologically under the names of the above-
mentioned authors, and the current 'received standard' English sounds set out in the extreme right-
hand column.

The changes between Chaucer's time and that of
Shakespeare, which will be seen in the following
table, are commonly referred to as *the great vowel shift,*

THE GREAT ENGLISH VOWEL SHIFT

An approximate summary in tabular form by Daniel Jones and C. L. Wrenn[1]

Words like	O.E. A.D. (1,000, Ælfric)	Chaucer	Shakespeare	Modern Southern
1. *Time*	iː (written i, í)	iː (written i)	əi	ɑi, ai
2. *Green*	eː (written e, é)	eː (written e, ee)	iː	iː
3. *Meat*	ɛ (written e, æ)	ɛː (written e, ee)	eː	iː
4. *Name*	a (written a)	aː (written a)	ɛː	ei
5. *Small*	ɑ (written æ, a)	ɑː (written a, au)	ɔː	ɔː
6. *Oak*	ɑː (written a, á)	ɔː (written o, oo)	oː	ou
7. *Food*	oː (written o, ó)	oː (written o, oo)	uː	uː
8. *Now*	uː (written u, uu)	uː (written ou, ow)	əu	ɑu, au
9. *Sun*	u (written u)	u (written u, o)	ʌ	ʌ
10. *New*	eu (written eow)	iu (written ew)	iu	juː
11. *Few*	ɛu (written eaw)	ɛu (written ew)	eu, iu	juː
12. *Know*	ɑu (written aw, áw)	ɔu (written ow, ou)	ɔu, oː	ou
13. *Way*	ei (written e3, ei)	ɛi (written ei, ey, ai, ay)	ɛi, ɛː	ei
14. *Day*	ɛi (written æ3, ay)	ɛi (written ai, ay)	ɛi, ɛː	ei
15. *Voice*	ɔi (written o3, oy)	ɔi (written oi, oy)	ɔi	ɔi

[It is probable that short i, ɛ, a (in closed syllables) and ɔ have not undergone much change.]

[1] Reproduced by the kind permission of Professor Daniel Jones.

Others of less magnitude which occurred later must be passed over here. Though the consonant-changes have been rather less marked, the spellings which represent them have undergone considerable changes.

Old English began by being roughly phonetic in its spelling. But in the four centuries of its written history (say from 700 to 1100 when the effects of the Norman Conquest began to be felt) this spelling inevitably became to a considerable extent unphonetic with the development of the pronunciation. For example, the *c* in the Old English words *cuman* 'come' and *cyrice* 'church' had approximately the sound of *k*, though the one was in the back or guttural position in the mouth and the other in the palatal or front. But by the end of the period the front *c* in *cyrice* had come to be sounded as a sibilant consonantal [tʃ] like the modern *ch*: and as the French scribes habitually used *ch* for this sound in their own language, Middle English developed the convention of using the letters *ch* for this sound [tʃ] generally. Again, the Old English *y* had the sound of [y]: but though this sound remained in some dialects, the French scribes wrote it *u* according to the use of this symbol in their own writing: and hence the spelling with *u* in modern *church*. But the French scribes found in English the usual spelling of the sound long *u* [u:] as in Old English *hūs* 'house' and the short *u* [u] as in Old English *lufu* 'love' to be always represented by the one symbol *u*. Thus it came about that they found themselves with the letter *u* doing duty for three distinct English sounds: [y], [u:] and [u]. Worse still, in the writing of that period the method of making the letters *m*, *n*, and *u* was such that they were very easily confused. To avoid such ambiguities in writing, French copyists gradually conventionalized the practice of using *ou* for long *u* as in *hous* [hu:s], and *o* for short *u* whenever it came next to *m*, *n*, or other possibly confusable symbols: so that *lufu* (which had weakened its ending to become *luue* with the medial *v*-sound represented by a second *u*) came to be written as *loue*. This is why so many words with the pronunciation of *u* have continued to be written, regardless of sound, with *o*; such as *love*, *monk*, and *son* corresponding to Middle English *loue* [luvə], *monk* [muŋk] and *sone* [sunə], which have become modern English [lʌv], [mʌŋk] and [sʌn] while retaining the now quite unphonetic spelling with *o*. Similarly, the French scribes had improvised a spelling *gh* for the then English strongly-sounded guttural *h* [χ] in words like *right* (Old English *riht* [riχt]) and *might* (Old English *miht* [miχt]): but these guttural sounds became silent in the later fifteenth century just when printing was becoming influential. Consequently we have a whole series of such words in which the *gh*-spelling may seem quite meaningless for pronunciation.

But enough has been said to indicate the nature of the unphonetic spellings which are a characteristic of English, whose roots lie far back in English linguistic history.

3. 'STANDARDIZING' OF SPELLING AND PRONUNCIATION

The formative period of Modern English Spelling was the Early Modern period, from the time of the first printers in the late fifteenth century to the reign of Queen Anne. Caxton (1422–91), who introduced printing to England from the Continent, printed from manuscripts as he found them, modifying the spelling sometimes somewhat indiscriminately from ideas of his own brought from his long service in Belgium. The *gh* in *ghost*, for instance, is perhaps an inheritance in English spelling from the Flemish in its initial letters. Caxton had spent most of his working life abroad, and his first successor, Wynken de Worde, was also a foreigner: and these foreign influences were to leave some permanent marks on English spelling. Caxton, who was in effect his own publisher and editor as well as printer, inevitably exercised some influence on printing conventions of spelling. But books did not really become widespread enough to influence the country as a whole till the seventeenth century; and so it was that the fixing of spelling by the printers proceeded rather slowly at first. Many Middle English practices which went out of date from the point of view of phonetic representation at the very time that the early printers were using them, came to be part of permanent spelling: and the sixteenth century, a period of greatest change in pronunciation, was just the time when the influence of printing was increasing markedly and the need for spelling-conventions was becoming apparent. The next century saw most of the present spelling established in printing, and a book printed in the reign of Queen Anne shews only relatively slight differences in spelling from that of the present time. It was in the eighteenth century too that the 'Gothic' or 'Black-letter' type used by the earlier printers finally gave place to the 'Roman' characters now used. The 'long s', ſ, which looks at first sight so like an *f*, was thus being replaced by the now ordinary *s*.

But it was the immense influence of dictionaries and the tendencies toward standardization which this signified as well as induced, that finally brought the definite acceptance of a permanent fixed spelling in English: and with the widening of education in the period since Dr. Johnson's great dictionary (1755) this has passed from the printers to the whole community who use writing.

Already in the early days of the Royal Society (founded 1662) a special committee had been set up to improve the use of English for scientific purposes: and Dryden, who was a member, greatly longed for an English Academy which might fix and arbitrate upon the usage of the language much as the French *Académie Française* had done. Swift, half a century later, shared this view; and when Dr. Samuel Johnson began upon his *Dictionary of the English Language* in 1747, he too thought that the language might be 'fixed' in an enduring best form as well as its spelling (though he became wiser by the time his task was completed). There was in the period between the Restoration and the close of the eighteenth century a definite tendency towards standardizing or working to a clear stylistic ideal in speech as well as writing. It was a time of grammarians and critics and of the rapid growth of dictionaries, and all these things made towards a closer fixation of spelling and the beginnings of a consciously standardized 'received pronunciation'. It would be an exaggeration to say, as has often been said, that Dr. Johnson's *Dictionary* fixed English spelling, for it was already by his time well on the way to fixation. But this great dictionary was the first to receive universal acceptance as the arbiter of usage and spelling. All dictionaries for the next century more or less imitated it, and the habit of regarding a dictionary as a final and indisputable authority in matters of spelling, pronunciation and usage, which is so widespread to-day, finds its beginning in the immense weight to the authority of the dictionary which Johnson's work gave. It is easy to see how the passing of the act of 1870 for universal compulsory education, and the vast increase of newspaper reading have strengthened the fixation of spelling. Even in America, where a few steps towards a more phonetic spelling in a few types of words have been taken, a fixed spelling on the same historical and phonetically out-of-date lines as in England, is universally employed.

The schools, which are compulsory, tend to foster a 'received standard' of pronunciation and to discourage the use of dialectal sounds and words, and the widespread habit of listening to broadcasting probably unconsciously produces the seeking after a 'correct' pronunciation. Indeed there has been some tendency to regard the British Broadcasting Corporation, which has sometimes had English language specialists on its committees for guidance in disputed pronunciations and foreign words, as a kind of incipient Academy which might direct the English language like the *Académie Française*. The founding of the *Society for Pure English* in this century, with its many valuable pamphlets on aspects of the modern language, is again a sign of the tendency to seek an ideal or standard of usage. Here it will be of interest to sketch the growth of dictionaries in England—a feature in which English scholarship has been a pioneer.

4. THE DEVELOPMENT OF DICTIONARIES

In the ancient classical world and in the Middle
Ages there were often made collections of 'hard
words' and foreign words with their meanings. These
are termed *glossaries*, or collections of *glosses* (a *gloss*,
from Latin of the Greek *glossa* 'rare word needing
special explanation', is a translation or explanation
of a word). Until the Renaissance such glossaries
were only selected groups of explanations and in no
sense aimed at the completeness we associate with a
dictionary. The Renaissance brought the need for
Latin and Greek dictionaries, and the impulse given
by the new attitude caused the thoughts of scholars
to turn also to the improvement and clarification of
the vernacular. So it was that crude and incomplete
dictionaries began to appear in the sixteenth century.
Such in part was Thomas Cooper's *Thesaurus Linguae
Romanae et Britannicae* of 1565, in which a number
of difficult or obsolete words are treated. In 1604
Robert Cawdrey produced a slim volume entitled *A
Table of Alphabeticall English Wordes*; and in 1658
Edward Phillips, Milton's nephew and pupil, published his *New World of English Words* in which are
contained, he tells us, 'the interpretations of all the
words derived from foreign languages'. The first two
stages of the history of dictionaries, then, were the
glossary first, and secondly the merely selective
dictionary which dealt only with 'hard words' or
those of foreign derivation.

The third step was the addition of *etymologies* to
the meanings of words: for to know the history of a
word before it entered the language is of value for the
understanding of its exact shade of meaning. Stephen

Skinner in 1667 with his *Etymologicon Linguae Angli-canae*, and the Dutch scholar Francis Junius (who first printed the oldest poem of the Old English Cædmon) with his *Etymologicon Anglicanum* in 1677, were the pioneers in providing etymological diction-aries for English, though both wrote in the then usual Latin.

All the foregoing were but preliminary stages; the first dictionary in anything like the proper sense of the word appeared in 1708. This was John Kersey's *Dictionarium Anglo-Britannicum* or *A General English Dictionary*. This embodies a fourth development, namely the attempt to set out the *whole* of the literary language. It was followed in 1730 by a much more scholarly work, Nathan Bailey's *Dictionarium Britannicum* or *A More Compleat Universal English Dictionary*, which included all the advances hitherto made in the science of lexicography or dictionary-making, but with greater fullness. Moreover it introduced slightly a fifth feature, the illustration of definitions and meanings by quotations from select contemporary authors so as to make much clearer than before exact shades of meaning by enabling the reader to see the words used in given contexts.

But the greatest landmark in the development of lexicography was Dr. Sam. Johnson's *Dictionary of the English Language*, completed in 1755. For this employed much more fully and effectively the method of illustrating by quotations which Bailey had only occasionally used. Moreover its definitions, despite some humorous or individual vagaries, were the first to be really clear, scholarly and effective. At once it became the standard work, for long the arbiter of English usage and the standard for English spelling.

H

All good dictionaries have benefited by its pioneering steps; and it set the model for the next hundred years, and also first set up the habit which has now become well-nigh universal, of treating a dictionary as a final and uncontestable authority. This habit is not altogether good, since dictionaries are always inevitably somewhat out of date, in view of the constantly changing nature of language.

It was Charles Richardson who, in his *A New Dictionary of the English Language* (1836), widened the scope of his illustrative quotations and first indicated a sixth development in lexicography, namely the inclusion of quotations to shew the historical uses of words (the meanings they had had in older times as well as their contemporary sense).

In 1928, as the result of seventy years of work and fifty of actual carrying out of an established plan, there appeared the final volume of The Philological Society's *A New English Dictionary on Historical Principles* published by the Clarendon Press of Oxford. This, the work of a number of editors and thousands of helpers all over the world, is the greatest scientific achievement in lexicography so far completed. It adds to the foregoing developments, the complete setting forth of the whole history and semantic development of every word known to have been used since the twelfth century. This it does by means of a series of definitions for each word, with a past history of its several different meanings which shew its exact development; and these are each illustrated chronologically by appropriate quotations from various periods. In addition, every known spelling the word may have had at any time in its history is recorded, together with a full indication of the current

British pronunciation in a phonetic script. It is thus, for the scholar, the most complete record of the whole of the English language, with all the material the student could want for the study of any and every aspect of its history. It occupies ten large volumes or twenty half-volumes: but for ordinary working purposes its material is summarized in two volumes in *The Shorter Oxford English Dictionary*, and still further reduced and adapted to speedier consultation in *The Oxford Concise English Dictionary*.

In America, Noah Webster was the pioneer with his *Compendious English Dictionary* of 1806, which follows well on the great work of Johnson: and in 1828 was published his *American Dictionary*, which was the foundation of the great *Webster's International Dictionary*, which is the universal working tool in America after successive revisions. *The Century Dictionary* (1889–91) is the great American example of a scholarly compendious English dictionary, in six volumes, which is largely an encyclopaedia as well. A *Dictionary of American English*, on the same lines (but reduced somewhat) as *The New English Dictionary*, embodying all of the English language that is recorded in America from the days of the earliest settlements treated historically, has lately been published.

5. SPELLING AND RHYME

A great revolution was brought about by the universal employment of printing in poetry by the end of the Early Modern period. For verse, which hitherto had been of necessity written to be recited and therefore heard, came now to be addressed more and more not to an audience strictly so called, but to a reader who might enjoy it in seclusion without ever hearing it recited or read aloud. Milton was probably the last great English poet who wrote with the deliberate aim of being read aloud. Now if the poet's rhymes, for instance, are no longer to be heard, but only received through the eye, an entirely new set of relationships between spelling, pronunciation and rhyme, will be set up. Rhymes may be addressed merely to the eye (*spelling*, or *visual* rhymes): or true rhymes which once sounded perfectly in accord may become quite lost with changing pronunciation while still remaining in the now fixed traditional spelling. The whole craft of verse and the poet's relationship to his reader is changed by the spread of printing. To an audience a rhyme must be recognizable by the ear: but to a reader a merely literary tradition of spelling or a merely visual resemblance may suffice.

We may distinguish the following five types of rhyme since the spread of printing. First, *true rhymes* which sound exactly alike still. Secondly, *traditional rhymes*: that is to say rhymes which were once true to sound, but which changes in pronunciation have rendered no longer exact. These have become traditional parts of poetic machinery and are accepted as good: as for example Milton's *hand* and *wand*, which rhymed in Middle English, but lost their correspondence with the rounding of the *a* of *wand* by the initial *w* in later Middle English. Thirdly, there are what may be termed *traditional spelling* rhymes. These are rhymes used by influential poets in past times which yet were never exactly correspondent in sound, but only in spelling, such as *love* and *grove* in Spenser and Marlowe. For these two words could never have rhymed exactly at any period of the language; yet they have become acceptable by a long tradition. Fourthly there are *eye-rhymes* or *visual* rhymes, which depend entirely on the agreement of spelling and have never become traditionally acceptable. These are usually found in immature or not very sensitive poets. Such was the rhyme of *foul* and *soul* in Milton's juvenile Paraphrase of the Psalms, though he became later a most exact craftsman of rhyme. Fifthly there are what I would call *true-plus* rhymes; that is, those in which the spelling of one or other of the rhyming words has been artificially adjusted to make a rhyme to the eye, even though the rhyme was already perfect. Spenser, for example, made the quite unhistorical spelling *arre* of the word *are* for a rhyme with *farre* (far) in which the spelling is quite historical as an archaism.

But to the student of the history of pronunciation, provided the safeguards suggested by a consideration of the foregoing points are kept well in mind, rhymes may serve as useful evidence in seeking to establish the pronunciation of a word at any given time, if one has a clear idea of how exact and sensitive a craftsman in rhyme a particular poet may be. These results may be checked by other kinds of evidence for pronunciation, such as the writing of English words by foreign grammarians, the opinions of contemporary specialists, or the divagations from the accepted spelling of less educated persons or the speakers of dialects. But this last must be used very cautiously, since so often the 'mistakes' in spelling made by most people have not been due to any effects from their individual pronunciation, but to all kinds of mechanical and psychological causes quite unconnected with phonetics. Let the reader examine his own occasional errors in spelling. He will find in most cases that they have nothing whatever to do with his individual pronunciation, but are caused by all kinds of associations unrelated to sound. Nevertheless, in past times when reading was less prevalent and traditions of spelling were less strong, the 'occasional spelling' may have real value as evidence for pronunciation when it is corroborated in some other way. Even now it may sometimes have its uses for this purpose.

6. INFLUENCE OF SPELLING ON PRONUNCIATION

If the English pronunciation has ceased, with the fixation of spelling, to have any effect on orthography, spelling has recently somewhat influenced pronunciation, especially with the immense growth of popular printing and the dominance of dictionaries. For example, *indict* [indait], in the received standard pronunciation, is already often to be heard as [indikt] because of its spelling: and *victuals* [vit|z] is often sounded as [viktjuəlz]. At the Renaissance a number of words of French origin were re-spelt as if they had come direct from Latin (the words *indict* and *victuals* are cases in point), and this produced an artificial spelling which later has sometimes come to remould pronunciation. Similarly, a village near Oxford called *Alvescote* was, according to inherited tendencies in local English pronunciation, called [ɔːlskət] thirty years ago: but to-day the local inhabitants, influenced by the Post Office and the printed form, have come naturally to call their village [ælveskot]. This tendency is by no means confined to the less educated:

and broadcasting announcers sometimes shew it. For instance, a number of words of Latin origin ending in -*or* unstressed, are pronounced in English with final [ə]: but we often hear announcers and public speakers saying *metaphor* ([mɛtəfə] in received standard) as [mɛtəfɔr]. St. Mary *Magdalen* had come to be pronounced by the sixteenth century as *mɔːdlin*: and this survives in the adjective *maudlin* which is derived from her name: but the spelling has caused the proper name, as distinct from the derived adjective, to be re-formed in pronunciation as [mægdəlin]. This time the received standard pronunciation has accepted the change: but the still living traditional pronunciations of the names of this saint's colleges in both Oxford and Cambridge, remind us of the earlier sounds. Chaucer tells us that the name of his Shipman's boat was *The Maudeleyne*.

CHAPTER IV

THE SHAPING, BUILDING
AND ORDERING OF WORDS. I

I. GENERAL CONSIDERATIONS

HAVING given some account in the last two chapters
of the vast English vocabulary built up from so
many foreign sources upon a native Germanic foundation, and of how its spelling and pronunciation
have grown up, let us now look more nearly at what
is still the core of the language, both in vocabulary
and construction, namely its native English elements.
Let us consider in outline how the shapes of words
have changed during the history of the English
language (and this must include the shaping of the
large foreign elements also in so far as they have been
assimilated), how new words have been built up from
elements already existing, and how the ordering or
arranging of these words has developed in the process
of time. The study of the shapes of words is sometimes technically termed *morphology*, from Greek
morphē 'shape' (though the same term is unfor-
tunately also used in the biological sciences and some
others in a different sense). The closely related study
of how the endings of words may be used to shew
their relationship is called *inflexion*. The study of
pronunciation indicated in the last chapter is termed
phonology, from Greek *phōnē* ('sound', or 'voice').
The whole subject of phonology or sounds, morphology or shapes, and inflexion, is sometimes called
(especially in German works on philology) *The*

Doctrine of Forms (*Formenlehre*). The study of inflexions is also known as *accidence*. The building-up of new words from already existing words, as *goodness* from *good*, is often termed *derivation* (the *deriving* or originating of one word from another). The *ordering* or arranging of words in the sentence is termed *syntax*, from Greek *syn* 'together' and *taxis* 'arranging'. But a glance at any text-books which treat, among other things, of syntax, will shew how difficult it is to draw the line between *accidence* and *syntax*. These two are very closely inter-related. For the way in which words are related in forming the sentence, whether by inflexional endings, prepositions, or the mere way in which they are ordered, must clearly often be at one and the same time a matter both of accidence and of syntax.

As has been said before, despite the vastly larger size of the foreign parts of the English vocabulary, it has remained, both in the fundamental simple words of its vocabulary and its grammatical structure, a Germanic language in which a continuous unbroken handing-on of its 'Englishness' can be traced right through from the first Anglo-Saxons to the present day. Naturally, therefore, English has never entirely at any time lost its native powers of making new words by derivation, of building-up words from native stocks and parts. Though these powers were atrophied by the centuries of foreign domination in cultural matters during the French supremacy, and to a less extent by the almost overwhelming importance of Latin at the Renaissance, they never ceased to be: and with the strengthening of the English tradition and its huge expansion in the later centuries, these powers have been to some extent called into use. Many new words have been formed recently from entirely native English elements.

Yet foreign tongues, especially French and Latin, have made their contribution to English word-building by means of new prefixes and suffixes which have in time become as active and usable in the formation of new words as the originally native elements themselves. Foreign words, too, have become so English in appearance as well as in sound as to have been thoroughly, so to say, 'Englished'.

Another formative influence on the received language, both spoken and written, in modern times has been that of dialect-vocabulary. A number of good and effective words have passed from this or that local or occupational dialect into the general stock, such as the perhaps originally West-Midland *dwindle* first recorded in Shakespeare, which may be a gift to English as a whole from his native Warwickshire.

As remarked in the opening chapter, one of the paramount reasons for the study of the English language, particularly by students of English literature, is the need for distinguishing the various shades of meaning and connotations which words have had at different times in the course of history: in other words the *semantic* or *semasiological* developments. The science of *semantics* or *semasiology* seeks to investigate the exact nature and the causes of change of meaning in words. Why should *presently* in Shakespeare mean 'immediately', but to-day any indefinite time in the future? The semantic aspect of words must be an indispensable element in full and true literary appreciation.

Yet it should never be forgotten that the written forms of a language are later and in some ways sadly inadequate means of expressing the personality. There must always be certain vivid and vital qualities in the spoken word that cannot be fully transferred to writing. One of these which is very important for most languages is *intonation*. *Intonation* is the relative pitch or tone of the voice in the different parts of the spoken sentence. What a deal of different meaning, for instance, can be expressed by the verb *do* by means of varying the emphasis and tone of the voice! Though this musical element in language has been somewhat obscured by the dominantly stress accent of the Germanic languages and their strong habit of placing the stress always on the root-syllable, English still gives an important role in its speech to intonation. It has its intonation-music peculiar to itself to some extent, as indeed have most languages.

The above topics, then, and kindred matters, will form the subject of this chapter and the next. We have looked at words, in a sense, externally hitherto: how they came into the language from abroad, how they came to be spelt and pronounced as they are. Let us now consider words somewhat more inwardly.

2. THE SHAPES AND ENDS OF WORDS

Old English (as used between about A.D. 700 and 1100) was never a highly inflected language, judged from the starting-point of the original Indo-European with its eight cases and its multitudinous verbal forms. Yet from the standpoint of the history of English and as compared with Modern English, it seems definitely to be a language of full inflexions. It distinguished four (sometimes five) cases of noun, adjective and pronoun by means of inflexional endings: it indicated whether the adjective was in the attributive or the predicative significance by means of separate sets of endings: it had in some of its personal pronouns a *dual* number, that is to say special forms to shew that only *two* persons were being spoken of: it distinguished the plural of its verb from the singular by endings, though without shewing in the plural the three persons separately. On the other hand, it had lost the separate expression of the passive voice which Latin, for instance, preserved from Indo-European, and this function had to be performed by means of auxiliary verbs much as in Modern English. Again it had only two tenses of the verb so far as simple form was concerned, making its others by mean of auxiliaries or contextual indications. But taken as a whole, it was relatively fully inflected. It even indicated four or five cases by the terminations or shape of its definite article. Prepositions, which may serve to shew the relationships of words in the sentence, were not nearly so much used as in Modern English, since they were not so much needed.

Like so many terms in the study of language which are convenient and traditional, but never quite exact, the word *gender* in grammar is well known, but difficult accurately to define or explain. In highly inflected Indo-European languages gender is said to be *grammatical*: but in a language such as Modern English, which has lost so many of those inflexional distinctions which formerly indicated gender (particularly in adjectives and pronouns), it has become *natural*. Grammatical gender depends on the *form* of a word and not primarily on its meaning. The three genders (from Latin *genera*, 'kinds' or 'types'),

Masculine, *Feminine* and *Neuter* (Latin *neutrum* 'neither') which are usually employed in treating of Indo-European inflected languages, are misleading in their names to a certain extent. For it is often the form and not the meaning of a noun, for instance, which determines its gender. Thus in Old English *wíf* ('woman'), *cild* ('child'), and *hús* ('house') are all neuter in gender, though *wíf* could not have been thought of as anything but female in sex. This conception of gender, then, in which one comes to learn to recognize from the type or form of the word rather than from its sex or absence of sex, is conveniently termed *grammatical*: for it is a matter of grammatical forms rather than of meaning in the accepted sense. In Old English the gender was grammatical.

The passing from Old to Middle English brought with it the transition from grammatical to natural gender. By *natural* gender is meant the classification of gender, not according to any formal principle, but to the sex or absence of sex of the noun, adjective or pronoun concerned. Since, however, generally speaking, only *animate* parts of speech (those which are conceived as having life) have the notion of sex attached to them, inanimate words have properly, according to the conception of natural gender, no gender at all. Such words are often said to be of *common gender*, while others describe them as neuter. But, in fact, natural gender really ignores words not having life in which the modern language gives no indication of gender whatever by inflexion or otherwise: and there is no need to pursue the matter. Personifications, of course, come under masculine or feminine according to their nature.

Middle English preserved a few traces of the former

grammatical gender, but these have almost entirely disappeared with the modern loss of inflexion. Grammatical gender can only remain a real distinction so long as there are inflexions, as for instance the indicating by adjectival endings or the forms of the definite article of the gender of qualified nouns. The confusion which followed, in the early Middle English period, the reduction of English inflexions, together with the great intake of foreign influence at that time, inevitably brought the break-down and disappearance of grammatical gender. In Modern English, for all practical purposes, the question of gender, since it has become entirely natural, scarcely arises.

Middle English is characterized by the reduction of the endings of words, or, as it has been conveniently called, the *levelling* of inflexions: and as a consequence of this, by the substitution of natural for grammatical gender. This process was rapid in some areas, like the North (where it had become marked even before the end of the Old English period) and the East Midlands; but much more gradual in conservative regions like those of the Southern counties and the South-West Midlands. In certain stereotyped phrases inflexional forms lingered into the modern period: but in general it may fairly be said that English had reached the modern stage of the loss of those inflexional endings which had been levelled in Middle English by the time of Shakespeare.

The following passages, taken respectively from classical Old English, early Middle English (late twelfth century), late Middle English (Chaucer at the end of the fourteenth century) and Shakespeare (the first collected printed edition of 1623), will give some idea of the relative proportions of inflexions and the general appearance of the language at various stages. It should be remembered that in Old English and early Middle English every vowel is to be pronounced.

Here is the beginning of Ælfric's account of the fourth day of the creation of the world as described in the Book of Genesis:

'On þæm feorðan dæge ure Dryhten gecwæð, "Geweorðen nu leoht"—þæt sind, þa leohtan steorran, on þæm heofanlican rodere—"þæt hie todælan mægen dæg fram niht, and hie beon to tacne, and tida gewyrcen dagum and gearum, and scinen on þæm rodere, and onlihten þa eorðan."'

In the following literal translation, words not derived directly from the Old English forms in the passage are Italicized:—'On the fourth day our *Lord* quoth, "*let there be* now lights"—*these are* the light stars in the heavenly *sky*—"that they may *separate* day from night, and may be as a token, and may work tides by days and years, and may shine in the *sky* and may enlighten the earth."'

The second passage is taken from the beginning of a religious poem of the late twelfth century copied at a slightly later date, called *A Moral Ode* or *Poema Morale*:

'Ich æm elder þen ich wes, a wintre and a lore:
Ic wælde more þanne ic dude: mi wit ah to ben more.
Wel lange ic habbe child ibeon a worde and ec a dede.
þeh ic beo a wintre eald, to yung i eom a rede.'

Here the spelling shews the typical early Middle English confusion, though slight normalizing has been made. The literal rendering, preserving, as before, all the words that have survived into Modern English, is as follows:—'I am older than I was, in winters and in lore. I wield more than I did: my wit ought to be more. Well long I have been a child, in word and eek in deed. Though I be old in winters, too young I am in rede (counsel).' Here all the words have survived.

Our third and late Middle English extract is the opening of Chaucer's *Epistle to Bukton* (a friend):

'My maister Bukton, whan of Criste oure kynge
Was axed, "what is trouthe or soothfastnesse,"
He nat a word answerde to that axynge.
As who saith "No man is al trewe, I gesse."'

Here, finally, is Macbeth's famous soliloquy before the murder of Duncan from the First Folio of Shakespeare in its original punctuation and spelling:

'If it were done, when 'tis done, then 'twer well,
It were done quickly: if th'Assassination
Could trammell vp the Consequence, and catch
With his surcease, Successe: that but this blow
Might be the be all, and the end all. Heere,
But heere, vpon this Banke and Schoole of time,
Wee'ld iumpe the life to come.'

3. THE ENGLISHING OF FOREIGN WORDS

We have seen in Chapter II how many foreign words entered the language as contributions, some temporary and others permanent, to the enrichment of the English vocabulary. Of all these foreign languages, which have been the source of the Modern English vocabulary, two, French and Latin, have for the most part been thoroughly assimilated to the native genius and pattern, as well as contributing a great deal in new suffixes and prefixes in the forming of new words: and yet both have continued to supply English with words and phrases which have remained in their original French or Latin forms. With Latin, Greek may be included, since most Greek words came into English through Latin. Such Latin prefixes as *dis-*, *pre (prae)*, *ante* and *post*, have come to be felt as parts of the English language, so that they may be used to form new words from already existing English elements. We have, for example, *pre-war*, *post-war*, *ante-date* and *disown*. Similarly and even more fully assimilated, we have French suffixes like *-ous* in adjectives from Old French, *-able*, *-ance*, etc., as in the words formed from existing native words such as *righteous* from *right*, *likable* from *like*, and *riddance* from *rid*. Then there are French noun-suffixes for turning adjectives into abstract nouns, such as *-ment*, giving *merriment* from the native English *merry*: and Spenser has used in poetry *dreriment* from *dreary*, and even *needment* from the noun *need*. Latin words often become Englished by means of the Old French suffix *-ous* just mentioned: and we may often distinguish an older borrowing by its having this *-ous* ending from a later loan which keeps the Latin suffix *-osus* as *-ose* owing to more conscious classical influence. Compare, for instance, *villainous* (in which the *-ous* is added to an English noun taken from French), *mendacious* and *rapacious* (in which the words on which the adjectives are formed are the Latin *mendax* and *rapax*), and *otiose* and *verbose* (where the adjectives are directly made from Latin *otiosum* and *verbosum*).

Latin technical terms and phrases, such as those properly belonging to the law which have passed into a wider circulation, are now often part of the special language of commerce, medicine, politics, etc. Such are *status* and *status quo ante* (with *ante* commonly

I

omitted), *infra dignitatem* (commonly shortened to *infra dig.*), *Deo volente* (hardly ever used other than as *D.V.*), *bona fide* (as in *bona fide traveller*), *prosecutor*, *executrix*, and *honoris causa*. But the Latin phrase formerly often heard in schools *mobile vulgus* 'the fickle crowd' had, already by the early eighteenth century, produced the abbreviated form *mob* which now sounds so utterly English though Swift complained against it. Indeed many Latin words have acquired so English a feeling that no one is conscious of their foreignness and sometimes few know them otherwise than as abbreviations. Thus we have *recipe* in cookery, which originally was the Latin imperative *recipe* in the sense of 'take' ('take so many ingredients'). In the days when Latin might be used for such purposes as medical prescriptions, the word RECIPE would be put at the head of the list of ingredients: and in the same way the word *item* is properly the Latin for 'likewise' used in such lists as accounts or prescriptions or recipes. The symbols *L.S.D.* for 'pounds shillings and pence' were originally for the Latin terms *libra*, *solidus* and *denarius*.

Again, English prefixes and suffixes may be attached to borrowed Latin or French words or vice versa, as *unjust* from *just* and *Frenchify* from the French suffix *-fier*, or *witticism* from *wit* or *vapourish* from *vapour*. Again, abstract Latin nouns ending in *-ion* like *condition* and *requisition*, have become concrete nouns and then had new verbs made from them, such as *re-condition* and *requisition*, and even the recent *de-requisition* (which, like *de-house* and *de-louse* may be merely an ephemeral malformation). But it may happen that an apparently unnatural hybrid becomes a permanent part of the language. From such words as the originally Greek *democracy* (*demos* 'people' and *krateia* 'rule') the ending -*ocracy* has become almost natural in English, so that what looks like a merely temporary word, *mobocracy* (so far only vulgar) can easily be formed. But from the French *bureau* 'office' the words *bureaucracy* and *bureaucratic* have been made: and these have seemingly become permanent.

Broadly speaking, it is those foreign words that are in common use and have a tradition in the spoken as well as in the written language, that become the most English in sound and appearance. There is a vast tract of language which exists for most people only in books and has no tradition in speech: and indeed many of these bookish terms have no tradition of any sort of pronunciation, since they only exist for most users of the language as symbolic groups of letters on the printed page. Latin, as the language of the educated classes for so many cultural purposes in the sixteenth and seventeenth centuries, developed in pronunciation just on the same lines (as to vowel-changes, for instance) as English; so that common Latin terms in the language came to have a real speech-tradition among the cultivated classes. But in the late nineteenth century there arose in schools a new way of pronouncing Latin brought over from the Continent and thought to be near to that of classical Roman times. Now the spreading of this new and foreign-sounding pronunciation has grown with the decline of general knowledge of Latin. For there has come a very greatly increased number of boys and girls in the schools who merely learn enough Latin to pass elementary examinations without seriously reading Latin literature or realizing it as a live language: and it is these who, having not enough knowledge to assimilate the tradition of Latin in English, unconsciously use the new Continental Latin sounds for words in English which they happen to recognize as Latin. Thus the English traditional *stratum* [streitəm] becomes [stra:təm], and one even hears occasionally *cinema* ([sinima]) spoken as [kinima] or [kainima] because the word was made from a Greek formation *kinēma*. Often the rhymes in English verse which depend on the traditional English-Latin pronunciation, are quite falsified by this practice.

4. WORD-BUILDING

As has been said before, English has continued to be able to make new words from native elements or from those foreign ones that have been so long in the language as to have become thoroughly naturalized. In recent times, particularly since the middle of the nineteenth century, this power has been markedly active. Perhaps the most outstanding method of making new formations of late has been that of using any and almost every noun as a verb. Thus such nouns of varying origin as *tattoo*, *drum*, *radio*, *ration*, *police* and the proper name *Banting*, have all also become verbs. The last-mentioned, because the final syllable -*ing* of the name of the famous physician Banting was felt to be like a present participle, dropped when the new verb *to bant* was formed. From the place-name *Shanghai* has been made the verb *to shanghai*, because this kind of act was first associated with the criminal life of Shanghai.

The converse process of forming a new noun from

a verb is seen in words like *run* (in cricket especially), *hit* (score a hit), *ride*, etc., where the new nouns have been made by using the verb-forms as nouns even though there were earlier words in the language which could have been retained for these purposes. A recent example is *broadcast*, where the noun has come from the verb, which in its turn has developed from an adverb *broadcast* (here the element *broad* is from *abroad*, with reduction of unstressed first syllable). Indeed examples could be adduced to shew that almost any part of speech has, at one time or another in the modern period, been used to perform the functions of another.

The modern development in the arrangement of stress, despite a relatively more fixed word-order than in earlier periods of the language, has made it permissible for new compounds to be formed more freely than was possible in Old English, though of course Old English could form them far more abundantly. But almost any types of words can, with the aid of stress-distinctions, be joined together in Modern English as new compounds. The importance in two-syllabled forms, for instance, of the distinction between *initial stress, end-stress* and '*even stress*' as determining by means of emphasis whether the forms in question are to be understood as groups of words or as compounds, will be seen by comparing the following pairs:—*a red cap* (even stress) and *red-cap* (initial stress); *a tóy gún* and *tóy-smith*; *óld áge* and *óld-age pénsion*; *lessór* (end-stress), [lɛsɔ'ːr], and *lésser* [lɛsə]. With the loss of most of the inflexional endings, stress inevitably plays a much greater part than formerly in the indication of shades of meaning. Consider how many divers senses can now be got

from the once simple verb *set* by means of compounding with prepositions or prefixes, and how the new
verbs thus formed may again become new nouns:—
sét úp and *sét-up*, *sét óff* and *óffset*, *setting the table* and
a new setting, *cróquet-set* and *sét of tóols*, *týpe-setter*
and *sétting-úp of týpe*, *set in place* and *ínset*, *súnset*
and *sét of a suit*, *set upon* and *set about*, *set up* and
upsét (verb) with *úpset* (noun), etc., etc. The vast
expansions of meaning which are recorded under the
word *labour* as noun and adjective in the *Supplement*
to the great *New English Dictionary*, will astonish
anyone.

The making of new words and compounds, the
using of old words as other parts of speech and the
reviving of older words with new meanings, these
processes are continuing as part of the natural life of
the English language: but what is remarkable is the
scope and variety of the methods of word-building
from native elements.

5. THE INFLUENCE OF DIALECTS

It was mentioned in the introductory sketch of the
history of the English language that a mixed dialect,
based on the habits of the educated Londoner, was on
the way to becoming the cultural language in the
fifteenth century, and in the early modern period
completed the process. It was also noticed how both
phonology and accidence in 'received standard'
English have acquired elements originally derived
from Northern dialects, which reached London as
influences indirectly through the East Midlands and
the wool trade. Such Northern influence is seen in
the accidence in the ending of the third person singular

in -*s* or -*es* of verbs, which replaced the Southern and South Midland ending in -*th* or -*eth* in the sixteenth and seventeenth centuries—first in the literary and then in the spoken language. *Has* and *calls* take the place of *hath* and *calleth*. Or again, traces of the Southern dialectal influences are seen in the predominantly East Midland type of London dialect in the initial *v* for *f* of the words *vat* and *vixen*. Had these words not retained this Southern feature of pronunciation (perhaps part of the underlayer of original South Eastern due to London's geographical position), we should have had *fat* and *fixen*: and in fact we often find in early Modern English the noun *fat* and its compound *wine-fat* (for instance in the 1611 version of the Bible). But with vocabulary, the influence of dialects upon the dominant cultural form of the language is much more difficult to define. For while differences in pronunciation among dialects are fairly well established by the work of investigators, little has so far been found out for certain about the distribution of vocabulary according to localities or dialects. Yet some influences from dialects can be discerned in the standard language of to-day.

Caxton, the pioneer English printer, sought to use the best and most suitable kind of English he could find, and based his practice largely on that of educated London. In him we find no properly Northern words: but in the years just before his time we see the first recorded occurrences in London writers of *busk* 'prepare oneself' (which has not survived outside of poetry), and *mirk* 'dark' (which remains as *murky*), and Chaucer had already used *crag*. These seem to have been Northern words (*crag* is ultimately from Celtic), and may have come in through East Anglia. Among commoner Northern words, *grovelling* (first as an adverb) and *ugly* had been used by London writers before the close of the fourteenth century. But though Chaucer in his *Reeve's Tale* shews consciousness of an accepted metropolitan dialect as opposed to those of the provinces, it was not till Elizabethan times that writers and speakers began to think definitely of an accepted English language for cultural purposes as against provincial dialects.

Especially through literature, in which influential authors sometimes deliberately chose to use provincial words, a number of words have come into English from other of its dialects: and some of these have been found to be vivid and expressive and so become permanent, or even reached the spoken language. We have already seen how the probably West Midland verb *dwindle*, which has become quite an every-day usage, was first recorded in Shakespeare: and the form *dwine* 'to pine' is still in use in Shropshire, being the verb of which *dwindle* is a kind of frequentative. Northern words in fairly wide usage in English are *gawky* (*gawk* from Old Norse *gaukr* is 'a cuckoo'), *irksome*, *fell* (noun), and *fond* (earlier in the sense of 'foolish'). From the West Midlands have come *dingle*, and probably *pother*. It seems that *charm*, in the sense of 'bird-song' (from Old English *cerm*) came in from the Central Midland areas. This last is only in limited poetic use, but is recorded in Dr. Johnson's Dictionary spelt *churm*: and Milton made most effective and deliberate use of it in a famous passage in *Paradise Lost* describing Eve waking at dawn amid the rustic surroundings of the Garden of Eden:—

'Sweet is the breath of morn, her rising sweet,
With *charm* of earliest birds.'

We cannot concern ourselves here with the vast
fields of new words that have been created or have
grown up in every kind of specialized or technical
department of language. Each occupational group
has its cant vocabulary, each new science or enter-
tainment-industry develops its own mass of technical terms. These are not part of the language
thought of as 'received standard', though it sometimes happens that some words pass from a limited
special vocabulary into general use.

6. DEVELOPMENT IN WORD-MEANINGS

It is natural that the general forms of words—even
although pronunciation is always moving—should
change relatively at a much slower rate than their
meanings: and hence the importance for the ordinary
student of the English language and its literature of
some knowledge of semantic developments. Consider, for example, how wrong the modern reader
would go if he were to take the words of the Prologue
to Chaucer's *Canterbury Tales* (quoted in Chapter II,
p. 56) as all having the significations they have to-
day. *Licour* (line 3) cannot be rendered by its modern
derivative 'liquor', nor can *vertu* in the next line
mean 'virtue'. *Croppes* does not mean 'crops', nor
foules 'fowls', nor *corages* 'courages', etc. The description of Chaucer's Knight,

'He was a veray parfit gentil knight'

is very far from meaning 'He was a very perfect
gentle knight'. For *veray* is the Old French *verai*

(Modern French *vrai*) 'true', *parfit* means something like 'complete' or 'finished', and *gentil* has its older sense of 'noble' which survives somewhat in Modern English *gentleman*. The line means literally, then, 'He was a true, complete and noble knight'. In translating from books belonging to earlier stages of the English language, therefore, we must especially beware of the dangers of what may be termed 'etymological rendering'—that is to say of taking all words that have survived in form as if they had remained quite unchanged in meaning. Such an attitude would imply the view that the language had remained static; which is obviously absurd.

It is clearly neither possible nor desirable in little space to attempt any sort of exact classification of semantic tendencies: but two opposing directions in which meanings have changed very frequently, may be indicated. On the one hand, there has been a tendency to generalize the senses of words, to make them wider and less restricted. Thus, for example, *presently*, since the seventeenth century, has passed from the meaning of 'immediately' to its rather vague and indefinite meaning of to-day. *Boy* in Middle English meant 'a rough unruly person', and has thus become very much wider in its modern application; while *very* (already mentioned in connexion with Chaucer's *veray*) was an adverb meaning 'truly', and has loosened its significance a very great deal in modern times as a superlative-forming adverb, though it keeps something of its original sense in such expressions as 'the *very* man I want'. In the traditional English rendering of the Nicene Creed the phrase *very God* exactly means 'true God'.

The second trend of semantic change is still more

marked in some respects: it is the narrowing or specializing of the meaning of a word of originally wide reference. *Deer* (Old English *dēor*) meant 'animal' of any sort till the sixteenth century, but is now limited to one particular species: and we find Shakespeare using it in both the older and the newer senses. Tom o' Bedlam in his *King Lear* says:—

> 'Rats and mice and such small *deer*
> Have been Tom's food for seven long year.'

Knight in Old English meant 'a young man' and was in use long before there was any technique of knightly chivalry: and *mere* in Old English could mean the sea or any piece of water. In a famous criticism of the pastoral in Milton's *Lycidas* Dr. Johnson wrote of the poem as 'Easy, vulgar, and therefore disgusting': but here *vulgar* meant something like 'commonplace', and *disgusting* only stood for 'distasteful'. Here, therefore, the meanings of *vulgar* and *disgusting* have not merely become narrowed, but have become different from what that statement would cover. This leads to the mention of a third kind of semantic change; that by which a word acquires a distinctly new meaning which is something distinct from a merely widened or loosened sense as well as from one that is just a narrowing. *Disgusting* in Modern English is something in meaning distinct from a mere defining or narrowing of 'distasteful'.

Cipher, for example, originally meant 'a numerical figure', but now signifies a secret code; *honest* meant 'chaste' (cf. the flower-name *honesty*='chastity') in Middle English and a good deal later; *still* in Shakespeare's time meant 'always'; and *naughty* implied in Middle English material worthlessness, later moral nothingness; and only from the eighteenth century the more trivial modern sense came into use.

It is always necessary to consider (*a*) the meaning of a given word in its period, and (*b*) its significance in its special context and author. This is particularly important for poetry: for the poet, in using words, is unconsciously drawing for their exact connotations on his own experience of life, and also upon all the associations and qualities of suggestiveness which all the poets whom he has read had put into them. Well has Shelley remarked in the Preface to his *Revolt of Islam* that 'he who is familiar with nature and with the best products of the human mind, can scarcely err in following with respect to poetry the instinct produced by that familiarity.' The student of literature must cultivate extreme sensitiveness to the finer nuances of words and their changing shades of meaning.

7. HOMOPHONES AND HOMONYMS

Words spelt differently but pronounced alike are termed *homophones* (from Greek *homos* 'same' and *phōnē* 'sound'. Those pronounced differently but spelt identically are called *homonyms* (from Greek *homos* 'same' and the adjectival *onumos* 'name'). Homophones and homonyms are especially likely to arise in a relatively uninflected language like English; but as a rule the context makes the chances of real ambiguity or confusion very slight. The homonyms *lead* (name of the metal) and *lead* (verb) are distinguished by pronunciation; and the homophones *red* (name of colour) and *read* (past of verb *to read*) are kept apart by spelling as well as in any conceivable context. But it seems to be a general rule that if there is a real danger of serious confusion between a pair of homophones, one or other must disappear from the language, whereas any confounding of homonyms is prevented by their differences in pronunciation generally. When homophones become so confusible as to cause real difficulty, there arises what has been called the *conflict of homophones*. For instance, the two words *queen* and *quean* (used until the later eighteenth century for 'a loose woman') remained both in common use till the time came when both were pronounced alike, in the late eighteenth century. *Queen* (Old English *cwēn*) was pronounced much as it is to-day from the late fifteenth century, but *quean* (Old English *cwene*) was sounded as [cweːn] in the seventeenth to mid-eighteenth centuries. They were thus kept quite apart in pronunciation. But *quean* came then to be identical in sound with *queen*; and the serious misunderstanding which then became possible brought about the disappearance of *quean* except in such dialects as continued to keep its pronunciation separate from *queen*. An Austrian Count visiting London in the 1770's is said to have abruptly ended his social career in the salons where he had played cards with the ladies, because he would persist in calling his *queen* a *quean*!

8. ARCHAISM

Archaism is the revival for special literary or other purposes of words which had become obsolete or had fallen out of use entirely (from Greek *archaios* 'ancient'). This practice, which is found to some extent in most cultivated languages, may serve, broadly speaking, either of two main purposes: it may seek to create a realistic impression of the right historical context by carefully using the words and style of a given period, or it may aim more vaguely at providing a romantic atmosphere for effects of mystery, poetry or the more romantic and impressionist aspects of history. Only for a period of history not very far removed in time from the author's, will it be possible for him to give an air of historical realism by the aid of archaic language. Where the period to be suggested is more remote in time, its actual language would be unintelligible and too difficult to reproduce; so that the *romantic* method of suggesting the atmosphere of a remote past by means of a few archaisms without special reference to period, must be employed. Or a poet may create the illusion of fairyland or the tone of an old ballad by similar means. Thackeray tried the realistic method in his *Esmond* to give the right historical atmosphere for the reign of Queen Anne; Scott in his novel *Ivanhoe* used the romantic method just vaguely to suggest an old-world background, since the actual language of his characters must have been the quite unreproducible Norman-French or Anglo-Saxon. Spenser used archaism to suggest the atmosphere of his *Faerie*, and Keats made a not ineffective attempt to give a slight impression of a document of Chaucer's time in his *Eve of St. Mark*. Such efforts as the above-named, and the occasional use by influential men of letters of archaic elements in their language, have at times left permanent marks on the literary language, and very rarely such archaic words have passed into the wider circulation of ordinary speech.

Spenser revived and greatly enlarged the meaning

for poetic purposes of the Middle English word *faerie* which had originally (from French) signified 'enchantment' or 'the place of magical beings': and the word, with all its new connotations, has become part of the language of romantic English poetry. On the other hand, this same Spenser revived for a particular description of a supernatural beast an old word in modified form as *blatant*. For his '*blatant* (he seems to have originally spelt it *blattant*) beast' this adjective was suggested by the old words Latin *blatire* 'babble', the French *blatir* and the colloquial sixteenth-century *blatter* 'to speak foolishly and confidently'. Now this word *blatant* has passed, with much change of meaning, into common spoken English as well as into the literary language. Similarly Spenser used the archaic coinage *derring-do* 'deeds of chivalry', from reading a passage of the fifteenth-century poet Lydgate imitating Chaucer, in which Chaucer's *dorring do* 'daring to do', had been misprinted as *derring do* in a context that made the words look like a compound noun meaning '*daring deeds*'. From Spenser, through a deliberate revival in Scott's *Ivanhoe*, *derring-do* has passed in Scott's phrase 'deeds of derring-do' into the literary language. Enough has been said to indicate the ways in which archaism has occasionally enriched the English language: but naturally this influence cannot be said to have been either very widespread or deep except in certain ephemeral aspects.

CHAPTER V

THE SHAPING, BUILDING AND ORDERING OF WORDS. II

I. THE ORDERING OF WORDS AND SYNTAX

GRAMMAR treats of the relations between the forms of a language and their meanings and uses: and it is usual to describe the treatment of *forms*—the actual shapes of the words (*morphology*) and their inflexions—as *accidence*, while the study of the meanings and uses of the material provided by accidence is termed *syntax*. Historically, however, *syntax* should mean 'the ordering or arranging of words' (from Greek *syn* 'together' and *taxis* 'arranging'). But such terms as 'syntax', inherited through Latin, like the other traditional names in grammar from the ancient Greek grammarians, are never strictly accurate. They have the advantage of general convenience and traditional familiarity, however; and there is no real gain in replacing them by arbitrarily chosen new terms which, while correcting the old inaccuracies, cannot but introduce new divagations from strict accuracy. Language, being a growing human product, can never be classified and set out with anything like the precision of mathematical phenomena.

But a little experimenting will shew that it is not possible always clearly and absolutely to keep the phenomena properly belonging to accidence quite apart from those which pertain to syntax. One cannot in practice consider each and every word-form without assuming or implying something about its meaning: form and function are so closely inter-related, as are language and thought, that one cannot strictly do anything with one apart from the other. The distinctive forms, for example, of the *subjunctive* mood which existed in Old English, had to perform also the functions of the *optative* (the mood expressing *wish*): or rather, the historically optative endings in the verb had come to be used also for the subjunctive. Consequently it is impossible to think of the typical verb-ending *-e* or *-en* in Old English without having also to think whether it is expressing the mood of thought (report or hypothesis) which we call the subjunctive, or that of wish which we term the optative. Only in relation to meaning and use can we treat of a given Old English verb ending its 3rd person singular in *-e*: we know that it cannot be the mood of fact (indicative) which would have a form ending in -eþ: but the form alone may equally well shew a wish or a reported statement or an assumption. Grammar teaches us the exact endings of the Old English verb: but syntax alone can determine whether a 3rd person singular ending in *-e* is expressing a wish and therefore optative, or an hypothesis and therefore subjunctive. Grammar treats of certain words, again, which have no meaning at all unless they are taken in a context, as, for instance, *and* or *the* or *at*; while syntax treats of the uses and functions of the conjunction (and), the definite article (the) and the preposition (at). But in fact the syntactician cannot begin to tell us anything about *and*, *the* and *at* until he sees or hears them in a sentence. Till then they are but empty forms: and only when he is given their context can the grammarian tell which is the conjunction, definite article or preposition. It will be

K

clear now that accidence and syntax must often tend to overlap, while at the same time there is enough real and convenient distinction between them to make the terms valuable as rough boundaries between different areas of grammatical study. It will also be apparent that the original and narrower definition of syntax as 'the arranging of words' implies inescapably the consideration of their meanings and relations to one another. We can only arrange words in the sentence in the light of the meaning aimed at, and at the same time the expression of that meaning by their fitting relationship to each other. Empty words like *and*, *the* and *at* are sometimes termed *kenemes* from Greek *kenos* 'empty' and a new formation *kenēma* 'a thing which is empty': and by contrast it is convenient to speak of *full* words as those which have some element of meaning even without any context at all, such as *dog* or *hunt* or *tired*. These latter *full* words have been also called *pleremes* (Greek *plērēma* 'something which is full').

Just as languages may be considered as either *living* (when they are still in active use and therefore alive and growing) or *dead* (when they are no longer actively spoken and living and have lost the possibility of growth), so too we may think of forms and groups of forms in a given language as living or dead. Living forms are those which still may produce new usages or developments, like the ending *-ness* for abstract nouns or *-ize* in verbs. Thus we can form new nouns ending in *-ness* from any new adjective that may come into the language, like the slang *browned-offness* from *browned-off*, or the verb *sovietize* from *Soviet*. Dead forms appear within Modern

English in a number of stereotyped or fossilized collocations of words, in which a once actively felt significance in a form has been quite forgotten, yet the word-group as a whole, inseparable through long usage, has remained meaningful. For example, in the phrase *I'd rather*, the *'d* of *I'd* is the shortened form of *had*, which in its turn had been reduced from a fuller form which indicated once the *subjunctive* mood of hypothesis. But English as a living language, except for a few fixed traditional phrases and usages, has lost the distinctive employment of the subjunctive mood, whose function is now carried out by the context. We use, similarly, the collocation *if I were*, in which *were* is the subjunctive, and feel it less satisfying to say *if I was*: yet in almost any other sentence we should use the indicative for the function of the subjunctive. In the proverbial saying '*the more the merrier*', *the* is in form a solitary survival of the old 'instrumental' case of a one-time demonstrative pronoun, and the literal meaning would be 'by so much more in number, by that much the more joyful'. The two *the*'s are 'correlatives' used like the Latin *quanto . . . tanto*, and *merry* in earlier times meant 'joyful'. But only a knowledge of the history of the language can make one conscious of the grammatical functions of some of the words in the above examples; yet they survive, as it were, as dead forms in a living context.

Again, we may look at a language in the light of all that can be learnt of its history—how its usages and forms have grown through the ages—or we may consider it as a thing in itself, as it lives now, concentrating all our attention on its facts of to-day, entirely apart from the causes that produced them or their predecessors. The historical approach is sometimes termed *diachronic* (Greek *dia* 'through' and *chronos* 'time') because it looks at a linguistic phenomenon through the previous ages that have made it what it is. This method often leads to a clearer understanding of the present state of a language. For, as language is a human growth, and is therefore always in a condition of flux, its present state can only be fully understood in the light of what went before to make it what it is. The method of approach which isolates the present state of a language and tries to study this without the possibility of any preconceived notions suggested by a knowledge of past history and causes, is called *synchronic* (Greek *syn* 'together' and *chronos* 'time'). It may be thought that what is often called 'objectivity'—the ability to see things as they in fact are, without any subjective feelings or historical prejudice—may be better had from the purely *synchronic* approach. Looking at a language as it *is* spoken to-day, without any consciousness of how one thinks it *ought* to be spoken or of what one would have expected, one is perhaps less likely to make mistakes which arise through expectations aroused by a knowledge of the history of the language or of what grammarians and philologists have written. But this method is necessarily incomplete: and it is desirable that the student of the living language of to-day should be able at the same time to approach it both diachronically and synchronically.

2. SYNTAX AND PARTS OF SPEECH

It is not proposed to attempt any systematic historical treatment of English syntax, any more than of English accidence. These matters properly belong to that branch of philology which is called *Historical Grammar*. Space only permits a brief touching upon a few of the more outstanding features in the development of the syntax of the English parts of speech. Yet it should be remembered that for the full appreciation of the living language in all its aspects, a knowledge of its history is always likely to be helpful. Nor, on the other hand, can we attempt anything like a full handling of the syntax of the English of to-day. That would mean, among other things, writing a descriptive grammar. It will suffice here merely to indicate some of the more significant points, emphasizing rather the *diachronic* approach, since the *synchronic* presentation of the living language is less likely to be unfamiliar to the non-specialist reader.

In the noun, only two cases have remained out of the four of Old English. The functions, nevertheless, of these cases still have to be fulfilled; and this is done by means of such aids as the wider use of prepositions and a more rigid word-order. Modern English has a Common Case which expresses the functions of both the old Nominative and Accusative; and the very same form of the noun is also used for the old Dative (though here a preposition often has to be called in to avoid that ambiguity which is always more likely in a language with but few inflexions. In the sentence 'He told the man a lie', Old English would have used a distinctive Dative form for *man* and another (the Accusative) for *lie*. But Modern English uses the same form of *man* or *lie* for the functions of Nominative, Dative or Accusative. But in the sentence 'He hit the man on the head', even Modern English must have a means of avoiding the ambiguity caused by the fact that there are no separate forms for Nominative, Dative and Accusative. Old English would have here put *man* in the Dative, and *head* in the Accusative, with no preposition. The one distinctive case remaining in Modern English is the *Possessive* or *Genitive*. But even this, distinguished by the ending *-s*, can for the most part in the spoken language only be used of personal or animate nouns. We say *John's book*, but hardly *the table's top*. For such purposes as that of the last phrase we normally call in the aid of the preposition *of*—*the top of the table*. In Old English the sentence 'The men from Canterbury came to the king' could be expressed ordinarily by using *of* in the sense now performed by *from*—*þa menn of Cantwara-byrig comon to þæm cyninge*. This use of *of* in Middle English spread, as the distinctive Genitive ending became less frequent: and this was perhaps helped by the somewhat parallel use of *de* by the conquering French. So we now say *the wall of the house*, and not *the house's wall*. Word-order makes all clear in the sentence 'He gave the king a book': and it would be unEnglish to say *He gave a book the king*.

Adjectives have lost all their distinctive case-forms as well as the separation of singular from plural which nouns still retain. Hence it is the word-order which must, with the aid of prepositions, indicate the function of an adjective in the sentence. Old English distinguished in the adjective, not only between singular and plural, but also four (sometimes five) cases, as well as special forms to shew whether the adjective was attributive or predicative. 'The good man' and 'the man is good' would have had different forms for *good*.

Personal pronouns have changed less in the matter of case-function since Old English times. Already *me* did duty for both Accusative and Dative, as it does in Modern English, for instance. Similarly with *thee*. *Him* has performed both functions since the fourteenth century. But in the 2nd person plural, the Accusative form *you* (Old English *eow*) has replaced the Nominative *ye* (Old English *ge*); so that this pronoun has only the one form *you* for all cases. Furthermore, this plural pronoun has throughout come—except in poetry and religious usage and in some dialects—to replace the singular: so that *you* is now both singular and plural. It performs the functions of *thou* and *thee* as well as those of *ye*. It has been remarked earlier that the Scandinavian forms *they*, *their* and *them* replaced the English forms in the Middle English period. But an exception to this is the survival of the native form in the colloquial *'em* which was in far wider use even for literary purposes until comparatively recently. This *'em* descends from Chaucer's form *hem* (late Old English *heom*), with the *h* dropped through lack of stress just as in *it* the *h* of the Old English *hit* fell out of use for the same reason. The apostrophe in *'em* is merely a printers' convention.

In the verb, the chief change has been in word-order—the entire cessation of the Old English practice of placing it normally at the end of the sentence. Old English treated the verb in this matter of position in the sentence much as German still does. This putting of the verb at the end of the sentence seems to have been the original Indo-European order. But so often in colloquial speech one adds a word or two after a sentence has been completed; as, for instance, in 'He came yesterday—the man I was telling you about' instead of the more carefully thought-out 'The man I was telling you about came yesterday'. This tendency was doubtless already present in late Old English: and to it we may add the danger of ambiguity or misunderstanding in a long sentence of which the verb only appears at the end. These and similar causes may have brought it about that the verb now stands as it does in the sentence. Emphasis and convenience have also played their part in changes of word-order of this kind. The chief change in the form of the verb—one which has produced a number of consequential changes—has been the virtual loss in Modern English of the Subjunctive Mood. Of course the two *functions* of the Old English subjunctive endings -*e* and -*en*—the expression of hypothesis and wish (properly respectively subjunctive and optative) —have continued in the language. It is only the *morphological* distinction which has practically disappeared. In Old English the subjunctive was regularly used for reported speech on the authority of the speaker, for subordinate clauses of several kinds, for exhortation and for the expression of wish. But, during the Middle English period, with the loss in pronunciation of the weak verbal endings -*e* and *en*, the subjunctive became mostly indistinguishable from the indicative: and it was natural that it should then gradually fall out of use except in certain stereotyped phrases and fixed formulae of writing. This was possible because generally it was found that no serious ambiguity resulted from the falling together of the forms of the subjunctive and indicative in nearly all verbs except in the 3rd person singular. Forms like *if I were you* and *if it be possible* survive because the indicative and subjunctive forms did not fall together so closely in the verb *to be*: but such expressions as *if he come* or *had I been there* only survive in more solemn, formal or poetic usage. Colloquially we should naturally say, for the last two examples, *if he comes* and *if I had been there*.

But the expression of wish, belief, etc., the originally optative form of the verb, which already in Old English had come to be a subjunctive as well, could not be always expressed without ambiguity without further help after the loss of the distinctive subjunctive forms. Hence the use of the auxiliary forms *may* and *might* to make periphrastic optatives. Thus where Old English could say *Ic gelēfe þæt he cume*, Modern English puts it *I believe that he may come*. Or (to give a more strictly *wishing* illustration), Old English could say *Ic wilnige þæt he cume* for the Modern English *I wish that he* MAY *come*. Indeed an auxiliary such as *may, might, should* and *would*, is generally used in Modern English to cover the ambiguity which the loss of the properly subjunctive verb-endings has entailed.

The development of the relative pronoun deserves special mention. Leaving aside some Old English methods of expressing the relative which have left no trace upon the language, *that* (Old English þæt) is the oldest relative pronoun in the language that exists. It was, as a relative, a sort of particle or indeclinable word without ever having had any sign of case. It was in common use till the Renaissance, when the newer *who* came for a time to be preferred for its function in the written language, partly owing to its similarity to Latin usage (where the relative and the interrogative pronouns have mostly identical forms).

This form *who* (Old English *hwā*) was in earlier times the regular interrogative. But, to avoid the ambiguity often arising through the absence of case-distinctions in the properly relative *that*, by Chaucer's time the Genitive *whose* and Dative *whom* came occasionally to be substituted for *that*: and then later the tendency spread to the Nominative, and *who* came to be used beside *that*. Thus from the sixteenth century, *who* was at the same time both an interrogative pronoun and a relative.

Side by side with the development of the interrogative pronoun *who* into a relative, the originally interrogative adjective *which* (Old English *hwylc*) came to be used as a parallel relative also: and in the sixteenth century we find *who* and *which* employed as alternative relative pronouns in literature, while the old *that* continued in full colloquial practice. Thus we find the Anglican version of the Lord's Prayer beginning 'Our Father *which* art in heaven', while the Roman Catholic *Douai-Rheims* rendering has 'Our Father *who* art in heaven'.

The Latinizing sixteenth century tended to exclude *that* from the higher literary language: but with the more natural desire to elevate the colloquial usage into literature exemplified in the later seventeenth century by writers like Dryden, *that* came once more to have a place of honour in the literary usage. Indeed so much did this seem an undignified lapse into barbarism to the classical Steele in the early eighteenth century, that he devoted part of one of his *Spectator* essays to a condemnation of *that* and an advocacy of *who* and *which* entitled *The Humble Petition of Who and Which*—in which the 'old' words *who* and *which* were made to complain against the new upstart 'the jacksprat *that*'. Since then it may be roughly said that both *who* and *which* on the one hand, and *that* on the other, have become almost generally interchangeable in good written as well as spoken usage, though *that* tends to be less acceptable when referring back to persons. *Who* is perhaps little more than an alternative to *that*, according to the needs of sentence-rhythm and balance. But a fairly clear distinction has sprung up since Dryden's time, by which *who* is used of persons and animate subjects, while *which* is restricted to animals and inanimate things. We can say properly 'the man *who* lives over there' or 'the man *that* lives over there'; but not 'the man *which* lives over there'. A restriction on *that*, however, is that having no case-forms other than its Nominative, we cannot give it a Genitive or Dative corresponding to *whose* or *whom*, nor to the equivalent prepositional *of which* and *to which*. We cannot say 'The man of *that* I was speaking' as an alternative to 'The man *of whom* I was speaking': but we must make a Genitive and Dative for *that* by placing the prepositions *of* or *to* after the pronoun and must have some intervening word or words. Thus, for instance, 'The man that I was speaking of' or 'The man that I was speaking to'.

Since Old English times it has been possible, especially in the North originally, to omit the relative pronoun entirely if the context makes the meaning sufficiently clear: and this practice has spread into the received language, particularly the colloquial. We say 'The man I met yesterday' rather than 'The man *that* (or more formally *whom*) I met yesterday'. Another colloquial usage that has somewhat spread into the literary language is the use of the Nominative

who for the Objective or Accusative *whom*. We say
'*Who* do you mean?', rather than '*Whom* do you
mean?' except when speaking very formally. This
tendency to use the more common *who* for the Objective *whom* is paralleled by a general spreading of the
use of *me*, *him* and *her* in emphatic positions where
strict 'grammar', based on Latin models, would
require the 'Nominatives' *I*, *he* and *she*. We say quite
correctly 'It's me' or 'It was her', or 'I knew it was
him'.

Finally, a few words on the present participle in
-ing. Old English had its own endings for present
participles (in *-ende*); and Middle English developed
this into *-inde* as well, with a Norse *-ande* in strongly
Scandinavianized areas. But an Old English form of
the verbal noun was already in use in King Alfred's
time ending in *-ing*, as *bīting* 'the act of biting' from
the verb *bītan* 'bite'. This type of verbal noun, in the
form derived from the inflected type which ended in
-inga, passed into Middle English. There, perhaps
partly through the influence of the genuine historical
participial ending in *-inde* (which was common in the
South and South-West), as *-inge* it came to be used as
the present participle ending as well as remaining
current as a verbal noun-form. Thus the later Middle
English *bitinge* (Old English inflected form *bitinga*)
was at once a participle and a verbal noun. From
this type the Modern English present participle and
verbal noun in *-ing* has grown to be the only form.
That is, historically, why such a word as *bearing* can
be at once the verbal noun and the participle. Compare 'He is *bearing* his burdens well' with 'His *bearing*
was soldierly' and '*Bearing* pain is good for the
spirit'.

3. INTONATION

In a language in which inflexion has been greatly reduced, word-order must become relatively more rigid. One consequence of this tendency to a fixed word-order will be an increase in the role of intonation in the language. For since the varying of the order of words is no longer so possible as a means of conveying shades of meaning such as those that depend on emphasis, this emphasis must be obtained by other means: and the varying of tone to indicate meanings no longer expressible by placing emphatic words in appropriate positions in the sentence (as is done in Latin) is one of the chief of those employed in Modern English. Moreover, in a language of the Germanic type with a relatively fixed stress, like English, musical variety of tone to indicate shades of meaning becomes much more natural. For these reasons such a language as Chinese, with the distinctions of inflexions, and even the whole scheme of parts of speech, completely removed, finds its natural way of development through a fundamental system of tones and tone-groups (called *tonemes*). A change of tone in Chinese will turn 'to buy' into 'to sell', for instance. In English, though the process of reduction of inflexion and its consequences has reached nothing like so far as the so-called *monosyllabism* of Chinese, and therefore intonation does not play so fundamental a part in the syntax of the language, intonation has, nevertheless, a very important and far-reaching role. A rising or falling tone in the parts of the sentence determines much of its meaning. Moreover, there is a very close bond between stress and tone or pitch, a strong stress, for instance, often corresponding with a rising tone. Such a sentence as 'You are going to buy that house' may be a statement of fact (*declaratory*) or a question (*interrogative*) according to whether the tone is falling or rising at its end. 'You are going to buy that hòuse' with the voice on a falling tone at its end states the fact: but 'You are going to buy that hóuse?' with a final high tone asks a question. Furthermore, other tone-variations in this sentence can easily be thought of which would make it express surprise that the house is to be bought and not acquired in some other way, horror that that particular house is to be bought, or a suggestion that some other type of residence and not a house should be bought: and this by no means exhausts the possibilities of intonation-variation in this one sentence. Or again, there are very many kinds of sentence, each with a difference of meaning dependent on varying the tone of voice, in which the verb *do* is uttered. A phonetic transcript tells only part of the truth about a passage of speech. For the full reproduction it would be necessary to have it recorded in a notation which shewed the various tones throughout—rising (indicated conveniently by a lengthened acute accent), falling (a lengthened grave accent may be used), level (a line horizontally drawn above the word is suggested), rising-falling (ᴧ) and falling-rising (ᵛ). Some find it more effective to indicate more fully the exact varieties of pitch in a speech by using a wavy line above the words, adjusting its height or depression according to the degree of raising or lowering of the voice. But enough has been said to indicate how important intonation is in Modern English, and how intimately it is linked with syntax.

Having now considered the English language from

the historical standpoint, the sources and methods of building its vast vocabulary and the ordering of its words, we may now appropriately ask ourselves how far any outstanding individuals may justly be thought to have contributed at all to its growth. This will be the subject of the next chapter.

CHAPTER VI

INDIVIDUALS AND THE MAKING OF MODERN ENGLISH

I. GENERAL CONSIDERATIONS

TO present a language in its entirety, it would be necessary to have, for any given period of its history, not only full phonetic transcriptions, but also, as we saw at the end of the last chapter, what may be called *tonic* transcriptions. We must have the pattern of tones as well as that of sounds, to possess a language completely. Indeed, it is the intonation, perhaps more than anything else, that gives a language its character; and each tongue has its own series of tone-patterns—its prosody, as it were. But it is only with the immediately contemporary speech that anything like this can be presented: hence the increase of late in the use of gramophone records, linguaphones, and other practical aids to the hearing of detailed speech-patterns. For the language as it has been in the past, however, it is only possible to judge by reading, sometimes adding some rough knowledge of its pronunciation from the statements of native grammarians or foreigners, by studying the occasional spellings of scribes, and from the rhymes of poets who were good craftsmen. There is no means of knowing exactly with what sort of intonation, for instance, Shakespeare would have declaimed his verse and prose, save a possible glimpse suggested by the study of the punctuation of his early printers which seems to have been based in part on rhetorical emphasis.

Bearing in mind, then, that we are, for the most part, necessarily confined to the written word in studying the past and the development of the English language, let us now consider one of the most interesting factors in its growth, the contributions that have been made to its vocabulary and idiom by individual writers of outstanding importance. Clearly this aspect of the study is not one of the basic factors; for no writer or group of writers can be supposed to have had any fundamental part in the shaping of any language other than one which is artificial. Yet there have been authors of such dominant literary influence and personality that their new words and individual phrases have become part of the literary heritage of poets and novelists and essayists—not to mention the more obvious journalists of late—and it has even happened at times that some of these literary additions and new turns to the cultivated language have percolated through to the spoken usage. One would be rash to assume that because the words *back* (a horse), *bump*, and the phrase *what the dickens*, are first recorded in the plays of Shakespeare, these must be Shakespeare's gifts to the language and propagated by his influence. For it may well be that he deliberately chose to use words and phrases from actual colloquial speech for his dramatic purposes, which had not till then appeared in writing. None of these are so individual as to merit the assumption of coining. But, on the other hand, there are expressions so vivid and seemingly individual in Shakespeare at their first appearance, which have become part of the literary, and occasionally also of the spoken language, that we are rightly inclined to regard them as examples of how an individual may contribute to the making of the language. Such phrases as *to out-Herod Herod* (with its many imitations), *patience on a monument, salad days, beggars description, foregone conclusion* (with a change of meaning from Shakespeare's), *conscience does make cowards of us all* (with again a change in the sense of *conscience*), and *brevity is the soul of wit*, have acquired a permanent place in the language.

Yet it is clear, however, that no individual writer, even with all the aids of popular printing, can permanently leave much mark on the language *as a whole* save in the giving of currency to some notable words and phrases. But in the field of poetry, influence is more easily exercised, since there is always likely to be some kind of a poetic tradition looking back to the great poets of the past. Much of Wordsworth's language is inconceivable without the influence of Milton, just as much of Spenser's is inconceivable without Chaucer. There is a sense in which Chaucer, though he could not have much influenced the language as a whole, must be thought of as a very considerable influence in the formation of poetic diction.

Some authors, again, have shewn special interest in the language, have criticized linguistic and stylistic fashions like Chaucer and Shakespeare, or have striven to improve it like Dryden, Swift and Dr. Johnson. The writings of such people among the greater authors, must afford at least information and examples of value to the student of the history of the language: and in the absence of the actual records of past speech, we must perforce study the growth of the English language through good exemplars of its writing.

When we look at the faces in old portraits, we are

often struck by physical differences in type from what we see to-day, though we cannot relate these to the ways of thinking and feeling of past generations which, besides these physical differences, must have separated them from ourselves. Looking at an Elizabethan, for instance, we get the impression of one whose physical make-up and mental processes were both considerably different from our own: yet we cannot form any idea of just what these differences may have been. But language, which is partly mental and partly physical, does remain, at least in its written form, to tell us something very considerable of Elizabethan ways of thought and feeling. We can, to some extent, check the impressions gained from a perusal of Elizabethan and Jacobean pictures and music, against the far fuller and clearer notions to be obtained by a study of Shakespeare's writings. In other words, language, which is a social activity, can, when studied historically, help us to the knowledge of important parts of our social history when it has been handled by its great masters. We may even be able, at times, to link up the evidence of Elizabethan physical and mental characteristics with what we may otherwise learn or surmise of Elizabethan pronunciation, since the act of speaking is partly physical, partly psychological.

Enough has now been said to indicate the value of some study of a few outstanding masters of the English language from the past, who have, because they were great as individuals as well as widely representative of their times, made contributions to the growth of the language as well as illustrating its characteristics at a given period.

In a sense every great author may be said to have

played some part in the making and the illustrating
of the history of the English language. But perhaps
the best plan in little space will be to take first
translations of the Bible, which have for obvious
reasons had a specially long and influential role;
secondly Shakespeare as being the greatest and most
individual writer as well as the most influential;
thirdly a few selected constructive working critics
like Dryden and Dr. Johnson, and lastly some notable
poets and orators.

2. BIBLE TRANSLATIONS

In considering the part played by various versions
of Holy Writ in the moulding of the English language,
one must try always to avoid the very easy confusion
of the influence of thought and image with that of
actual word and phrase. For example, it has often
been said that St. Paul's notable image 'sounding
brass or a tinkling cymbal' in the opening of I Corinthians, chap. 13, shews a wonderful skill in the
English translators. But when we consider the Latin
aes sonans aut cymbalum tinniens from which the early
translators like Wyclif (whom here the Authorized
Version of 1611 is following at a long distance) had
to make their renderings, we can see that there was
really very little choice of words, and that the virtue
of the passage is in the image itself, which was the
invention of St. Paul: so that even when the reform-
ing translators had the Greek of St. Paul before them,
they could not improve on what the Latin had already
yielded. On the other hand, Tyndale's 'Babble not
much' for the Greek *mē battalogēsēte* was a better
rendering of a difficult expression (Matt. VI, 7) than

the Authorized Version's 'Use not vain repetitions':
yet it is the latter rendering which has remained in
the literary language, while the word *babble* has continued in the colloquial use in which Tyndale found it.

While the Authorized Version, made by direction of
King James I in 1611, has been the great influence in
phrase-making, almost all the earlier versions of the
Modern English period have left their mark. But it
is also noteworthy that the Anglican Prayer-book
(first issued in 1549 and finally revised in 1662) has
shared to no small extent the kind of influence most
easily attributable to the King James's translation.
In The Lord's Prayer, for instance, as recorded by
St. Matthew, the Authorized Version has 'Forgive us
our *debts*' (Matt. VI, 12) following the 'received text'
of both Latin and Greek: but the Anglican Prayer-
book, taking its rendering from Tyndale's New Testament completed by extension in 1534, has 'Forgive
us our *trespasses*'. This is not the place to discuss the
origin of the rendering *trespasses* (*trespas* is a word
from Old French found in English as early as the
beginning of the thirteenth century), which corre-
sponds to the French version 'Pardonnez-nous nos
offenses' as against the equivalent of *debts* in most
other languages. The point is that the effect of this
version has been to give an altogether wider currency
to the originally purely legal term *trespas*. Again, the
now quite ordinary word *scapegoat* came for certain
into currency through its coinage by Tyndale in
translating a Hebrew term which he had not fully
understood (Levit. XVI, 8). The phrases *Prodigal
son* and *mess of pottage*, which are generally recognized as Biblical, came into the language in fact not
through any rendering of Scripture, but through

chapter-headings in pre-Authorized Version Bibles. The well-worn phrase *sweat of thy brow* (and its imitations) cannot be found in any extant version of the Book of Genesis (III, 19), where all seem to agree on 'sweat of thy *face*': and one must suppose that the expression has somehow survived from one of those Lollard versions of the Bible which existed and disappeared during the fifteenth century.

Tyndale, who seems to have hated 'poetry', had a genius for the telling phrase and the idiomatic yet beautiful rendering: and a vast deal of his phraseology has remained part of the language through its having been taken over unchanged by King James's translators. That is partly why the great influence of the Bible upon the English language has been as a phrase-maker. A few words and phrases have come from the apparent inventions of Biblical translators, apart from the Authorized Version: like Tyndale's *scapegoat* already mentioned, Coverdale's *tender-hearted* (2nd Chron. XIII, 7) and *loving kindness* (Psalm 89, 33), the Calvinists' Geneva version (1560) in the matter of the *mess of pottage* noticed above, or the phrase *the iron hath entered my soul* from the *Douai-Rheims* Bible of the Jesuits. But it is in its phrases, and also to some degree in its prose-rhythm and syntax, as well as in the less definable regions of style, that the Authorized Version has remained a dominant influence on the literary language, and through **it at** times even on the language of ordinary talk.

It is natural in most peoples that the language of sacred truths should be a little archaic, a little removed from the usage of the daily round of life, a little suggestive of mystery, and so should use a good deal of symbolizing imagery. King James's translators were therefore on sound ground in choosing to make their English a little archaic for the time and to replace some of Tyndale's more colloquial usages by a more dignified parlance. Tyndale, in a moment of controversial zeal, had claimed to be able to make the plough-boy know more theology than a certain priest of Gloucester by means of his English version of the Bible: but one needs a more remote and more dignified language for some aspects of divine revelation, as well as the strength in language which tradition may have given to some sacred words. The Authorized Version translators seem to have seen these points, and with characteristically English genius, steered in their language a course which was a compromise between the extreme attempts at literalness and the colloquialism sometimes found amid Tyndale's wealth of just-right phrases, and the clinging to tradition and Latin terms which often marked the early Roman Catholic version. It is possible that it was because of the slightly archaizing tendency of the Authorized Version that a few words which were becoming obsolete at the time were revived and made permanent in the language, such as *damsel* and *raiment*. But it may equally well be thought that these and similar words owe their revitalizing about this time to the widely increasing popularity of romances such as Malory's *Morte d'Arthur* in the sixteenth century.

It is particularly in the Old Testament that Tyndale's gift for phrasing has passed by way of the 1611 Bible into the language. A glance at the last chapter of Ecclesiastes, in which Tyndale had excelled in finding the right rendering of the beauty and

strength of the Hebrew poetry, will shew how much
Tyndale was a maker of English. The now familiar
phrases from the Authorized Version: *the burden and
heat of the day* (Matt. XX, 12), *eat, drink and be merry*
(Luke XII, 19), *the powers that be* (Romans XIII,1)
and *the fatted calf* (Luke XV, 23), are all the work of
Tyndale. His attempts at a literal following of the
Greek in certain technical terms of religion to get rid
of what he supposed were later superstitious connotations, were mostly replaced in the Authorized Version
by the traditional English words: and his implied
assumption of the unchanging meanings of such
words suggests a static view of language not properly
thought out. Of this type was his writing of *senior* or
elder for *priest* (Greek *presbyteros*), *congregation* for
church (Greek *ecclēsia*) and *favour* for *grace* (Greek
charis). But before he died he had begun in his
revisions to replace some of these by the traditional
words, and had returned to the familiar *full of grace*
for his earlier *highly-favoured* in the Annunciation
(Luke I, 28), though the Authorized Version did not
endorse his second thoughts here. On the other hand,
much of the vast enrichment of meaning in the
English word *charity* has come from its restoration,
as against Tyndale's *love* (Greek *agapē*, Latin *caritas*),
in the famous passage in I Corinthians XIII. In
Luke VII, 22, where the Vulgate, literally following
the Greek, has *pauperes euangelizantur*, the Authorized Version, following Tyndale's method, has 'to the
poor the *Gospel* is preached': but in the more imaginative form in which he had left it—'to the poor is
the *glad tidings* preached'—Tyndale gave to the
language the phrase *glad tidings* which has remained
valuable and familiar.

The mere habit of listening every Sunday to portions of the Bible, even in a semi-somnolent or inattentive state, has the effect of causing much of its phrasing and rhythm to become part of one's mental make-up, so that it comes up quite unsought at all kinds of occasions. This is proved by the vast influence of the Bible on English prose-rhythm and phrasing, as well as on the many images and verbal echoes which have continued to owe their origin to the Bible translations long after men have ceased to know it well or to imitate it deliberately. The written language, especially that of the more facile kinds of composition, continues to be riddled with phrases and images and new formations modelled upon these, which come not directly from the Bible, but from those strata in the English language which owe their first existence to the Authorized Version and its predecessors. Even the spoken language retains something of these tendencies. The man who says 'I wash my hands of the whole business', is unconsciously echoing an image which came into the language of his forebears through familiarity with the account of Pilate's action of washing his hands in public (Matt. XXVII, 24). Or consider the vulgar expression *gone to kingdom come*, which must somehow have been suggested by the Lord's Prayer. The phrase *cared for none of those things* comes from the account of Gallio in Acts XVIII, 17, and *common or unclean* comes from Acts XI, 8. The vast influence of Biblical names and stories is, however, rather a matter of cultural history than of language proper: and such material belongs mostly to Common European culture rather than to English in particular. In the matter of Biblical English phraseology, it is significant to note that in the following two verses (Chap. II, 11 and 12) of The Song of Solomon in the Authorized Version, two phrases occur which are familiar as a part of the literary language, neither of which is any longer known by even most educated people to come from the Bible:—'For lo, the winter is past, *the rain is over and gone*; the flowers appear on the earth; the time of the singing of birds is come, and *the voice of the turtle* is heard in our land.' The phrase *the rain is over and gone* occurs, for instance, in Wordsworth's *Lines Written in March* unnoticed by almost anyone as an echo: and when a recent American play was entitled *The Voice of the Turtle*, very few of those who saw it connected the image with The Song of Solomon.

3. SHAKESPEARE'S INFLUENCE

The influence of Shakespeare as a 'maker of English' is very much of the same kind as that of Bible translations, though naturally its incidence, despite undoubted colloquial usages and almost endless literary echoes and poetic assimilations, has not been so fundamental or so widespread. We are not here concerned with the fact that ever since his own time, Shakespeare has been the master and the source, often not consciously used, of countless playwrights, poets, prose-writers and popular journalists. It is only with the Shakespearean sources of actual parts of the general literary and spoken language that we have to do here.

Shakespeare was immensely interested, like Chaucer, Milton, Wordsworth and many more poets, in the English language. He constantly criticizes or satirizes linguistic and stylistic fashions among his contemporaries, while himself experimenting with all kinds of innovations, dialectal adaptations and archaisms. The 'Italianate Englishman' of his time is referred to in *As You Like It*, IV, 1, 35 ff.:—Rosalind addresses Jaques, who had boasted of being a traveller, thus:

> 'Farewell, Monsieur traveller: look you lisp, and wear strange suits . . . or I will scarce think you have swam in a Gondola.'

In *Love's Labour's Lost*, we find a pedantical Latinizing schoolmaster Holofernes, the Curate Sir Nathaniel and the 'fantastical Spaniard' Don Armado, all exhibiting fashionable linguistic aspects to be ridiculed: and Berowne finally discovers the value of 'plain honest words' and addresses his love in the following terms of linguistic renunciation (V, 2, 403 ff.):—

> 'O Never will I trust to speeches penn'd,
> Nor to the motion of a school-boy's tongue,
>
> .   .   .   .   .
>
> Nor woo in rhyme like a blind harper's song,
> Taffeta phrases, silken terms precise,
> Three-pil'd hyperboles, spruce affection.'

Affection here has the sense of 'affectation'. In *Henry IV Part I* (II, 4) we find elaborate satire of the style of 'Euphues' and of some popular tragedies. In *Hamlet* (II, 2, 533 ff.) the apparently Warwickshire dialect-word *mobled* in the phrase *mobled queen* is commented upon by Polonius: and indeed the whole play abounds in references to all kinds of affectations in language. That Shakespeare was very language-conscious is evidenced almost everywhere in his plays, as for instance by the many puns and equivocations which are found especially in his earlier works. Thus the pun in *Hamlet* (III, 2, 250) on the words *trap* and *tropically* depends entirely on the then current pronunciation of the *o* of *tropically* as an *a*, so that it easily connected in the mind with *trap* when heard.

As an experimenter with the dramatic use of dialect, Shakespeare was remarkable; and in so doing he made some permanent contributions to the English language. In early life he tried to suggest 'local colour' in *The Taming of the Shrew* (Induction) by making Christopher Sly use some provincialisms, notably the probably Warwickshire word *pheeze* 'to drive away' and hence 'to settle the business of'. The rustical rhymes of Touchstone in *As You Like It* and of the Fool in *King Lear* use some deliberate provincialisms very effectively to gain the required atmosphere. In later plays we occasionally find dialect words employed for poetic effect, like the *blood-bolter'd* Banquo of *Macbeth* (IV, 1, 123) in the sense of 'with blood in his matted hair', in which the *bolter'd* looks like a definitely West Midland word. In *Henry V* we find Shakespeare entertaining his audience with a very successful attempt at the dialects of Scots, Irish and Welsh soldiers of the English army, as well as an Englishman learning French. In *The Merry Wives of Windsor* we have the English of the Frenchman Dr. Caius as well as the masterly Welshman's English of Sir Hugh Evans. But we find a more generally significant achievement in the rustical dialect of Edgar disguised as a peasant in *King Lear*. For here Shakespeare is using in an early example that convention, which became fairly widespread, of making the stage rustics speak a kind of modified South-Western. To be effective on a

London audience, such a rustic must use a dialect
not too remote for intelligibility, and odd enough to
sound comic: and here there is a general air of
provincialism, a few South-Western characteristics
(with some others that come from other provincial
areas), but nothing in the vocabulary that a Londoner
would not understand. In short, it is a literary or
stage dialect, not a real one. It is in a sense the
ancestor of much both on the stage and in the novel,
though not the first in its kind. Perhaps his native
Warwickshire suggested the contemptuous term for
a Foreigner (still said to be heard in the Birmingham
area in a slightly changed form) *basimecu* (*Henry VIII
Part II*, IV, 7, 31) and the idiomatic phrase *speak
within door* meaning 'speak as quietly as possible'
(*Othello*, IV, 2, 144). In all this dialect-material, the
one word that seems to have come into both general
literary and spoken use through Shakespeare is the
probably West Midland *dwindle* already mentioned,
in the phrase (*Macbeth*, I, 3, 23) *dwindle, peak and
pine*. *Dwindle* is a frequentative of *dwine* (Old
English *dwīnan* 'pine') which latter is still in use in
Shropshire. *Peak* in this quotation in the sense 'waste
away' is also probably Western, but it only survives
in the form of the adjective of our colloquial
language *peaky*.

Besides using a number of archaisms for poetic
effect on occasion, as did many other Elizabethans,
Shakespeare may have made a special effort to frame
it to the suggestion of a time two centuries earlier in
the Gower choruses in *Pericles* with its stylistic air of
antiquity and a few archaic words: but this effort
seems more like that of another hand in this only
partially genuine Shakespearean play. Sometimes

Shakespeare makes fun of the archaizing tendency of his time, as in Pistol's speech to Bardolph on his wishing to become a tapster instead of a soldier:

'O base Hungarian wight, wilt thou the spigot wield?'

(*Merry Wives of Windsor*, I, 3, 21) and in a number of passages the archaic *eyne* for *eyes* is used for the sake of the rhyme or for comic effect, as in

'If the scorn of your bright eyne
Have power to raise such love in mine'

(*As You Like It*, IV, 3, 51–2). But as Shakespeare is primarily a playwright, archaism, save for rare occasions, is not an important part of his style.

Mention has already been made of the fact that a number of words first seem to make their appearance in Shakespeare. But unless there is special reason to regard these as individual creations, it is better to take all colloquial terms, at any rate as more likely to have been lifted out of the spoken language for dramatic purposes. Similarly, Latin words found for the first time in Shakespeare, unless of special individual quality, are more likely to have accidentally first been recorded in his works. Thus *bump* from the spoken language, and *castigate* from Latin, are scarcely likely to have been coined in English by Shakespeare; nor are *gloomy* (found at about the same time in Marlowe's *Edward II* and Shakespeare's *Titus Andronicus*), *auspicious* and *critic*. Shakespeare has been shewn to have surpassed all other poets in the vastness and variety of his vocabulary: but this does not mean that the considerable number of words first recorded in his plays are all his coinages. On the other hand, in the following famous passage from

Macbeth (II, 2, 61–3) the word *incarnadine* seems so individual in its context as to suggest (this being its first occurrence) a Shakespearean creation:—

'Will all great Neptune's ocean wash this blood
Clean from my hand? No, this my hand will rather
The multitudinous seas *incarnadine*,
Making the green one red.'

But it is more in the making of new compounds and especially in the creation or adaptation of apt or beautiful phrases from the spoken idiom, that Shakespeare can be looked upon properly as an individual contributor to the making of Modern English. With the French original prefix *en* (or *em*) he made a number of new words, such as *enact* (which seems to derive its currency from his use of it), *embattle* 'draw up in order of battle', *embay'd* 'locked in a bay' *empoison*, *enchafed* 'excited', *enchas'd* 'adorned', *endeared* 'increased in value', *enfree*, *engaol*, *engild* 'brighten with golden light', *engirt*, *enkindle* (metaphorically), *enlink*, *enmesh* (perhaps current as *emmesh* because of Shakespeare), *enrooted*, *enseamed* 'loaded with grease', *ensky* and *entame*. By joining one adjective with another he made new effective poetic compounds like *daring-hardy* and *happy-valiant*. He used some adjectives to make new verbs, such as *happy* 'to make happy' (Sonnet, VI, 6), and *safe* 'to make safe' (*Antony and Cleopatra*, I, 3, 55). From nouns he takes the verbs *spaniel'd* 'followed like a spaniel' (*Antony and Cleopatra*, IV, 10, 34, if Hanmer's universally accepted emendation stands) and *childed* and *father'd* both in the one passage in *King Lear* (III, 6, 119). With the prefix *un-* he has the compounds *unavoided* 'inevitable', *unvalu'd* 'precious beyond valuation', *unbless*, *unbody*, *uncharge* 'acquit', *uncolted*, *unexpressive* 'inexpressible', *unfather'd*, *unfellow'd* 'without an equal', *ungot* 'unborn', *unhair*, *unkiss*, *unroosted* 'ousted from one's place', and many more.

But it is in a multitude of phrases above all else, and in imitations or misunderstandings of them, that Shakespeare's language may be said still to live in the full sense of the word. It is here that his chief contribution to the language is to be found.

Like other dramatists of the period, Shakespeare used plenty of material from colloquial and 'low' parts of the language. But he stands out in his use of this for the individuality of his effects. It may be, too, that some of his transfers of words and phrases from the spoken to the written language have kept alive usages that would otherwise have disappeared like so many ephemeral fashions in language. For example, the still familiar *what the dickens* first is recorded in *The Merry Wives of Windsor* (III, 2, 20) in a speech of Mrs. Page beginning 'I cannot tell what the dickens his name is'. The likely connexion of *dickens* here with *Dickon*, a word for a boy mischief-maker recorded a little earlier in the play *Gammer Gurton's Needle*, suggests that the phrase was one of that kind meaning 'what the devil' in which the name of the evil one is avoided in a euphemism which has lost its exact form. It is at least a permissible speculation that we may owe the survival of *what the dickens* to Shakespeare just as we do the word *dwindle*, and to set these beside the score of telling phrases of a more dignified kind which his genius has made or made lasting.

Very few indeed outside the ranks of professional

students are aware that in the expression *past praying for* they are using a phrase first heard (as far as our knowledge goes) on the lips of Falstaff in *Henry IV Part I* (II, 4, 215), or that *patience on a monument* is first known from *Twelfth Night* (II, 4, 116) in Viola's description of a girl pining away through unrevealed love:—

> 'She sat like patience on a monument,
> Smiling at grief.'

To the manner born, like a particularly large number of Shakespeare's permanently English phrases, is from *Hamlet* (I, 4, 15), as is also *hoist with his own petard* (III, 4, 207) meaning 'blown up by his own bomb'. *Caviare to the general*, where *general* means 'the common multitude' (II, 2, 466), and *to be or not to be*, are again specimens of different types of now well-used phrases provided first in *Hamlet*. Indeed, a film production of *Hamlet* in a shortened form recently struck some critics as something like a recitation of clichés: so full of phrases that have now become part of the machinery of literature and journalism is this play.

Some of Shakespeare's phrases have remained in currency among those who are innocent of any knowledge of the playwright, and are found even in accepted parlance with a meaning other than that which Shakespeare had intended. The most startling of these is perhaps *a foregone conclusion* first found in *Othello* (III, 3, 429), where the meaning is 'an experience previously undergone': for a fairly common sense of *conclusion* was then 'experiment' or 'experience', which does also survive in the Shakespearean phrase *to try conclusions* from *Hamlet* (III, 4, 195). Another

M

commonly misapplied phrase from *Hamlet* is *more honour'd in the breach than the observance*: for as employed by Hamlet (I, 4, 15) it refers to the Danish custom of very heavy drinking, upon which he comments that the custom would be more honourably broken than observed.

Elizabethan and Jacobean English was characterized by a most marked increase of flexibility in its grammatical usages, as men came to feel that the freedom of the individual suggested by the Renaissance had its expression in the use of language. New collocations of words in which nouns or adjectives might perform the functions of verbs, came into use; so that some careless explorers have even been led into thinking that Elizabethan, and therefore Shakespearean English, had no 'grammar' at all. This is an exaggeration and a misunderstanding; but it is true that the Elizabethans often seem to be able to interchange the functions of noun, adjective and verb in a way which seems logical rather than grammatical in forms where the loss of inflexions has removed the morphological differences. Shakespeare used this flexibility to the full. As he was the first great writer of the widest interest and influence after the loss of the English inflexions, it may be that his practice has had its effect in encouraging the extraordinary flexibility of Modern English grammar, as distinct from the relative fixity of its word-order.

4. SOME FORMATIVE WORKING CRITICS

It is generally true that great users of the language, whether writers or public speakers, have been language-conscious and have taken keen and critical interest in the medium they worked in. We have seen how this was very clearly so of Shakespeare. The translators of the Authorized Version of the Bible must be thought of as a group working closely together. But though we cannot know of their individual views or their criticisms of the language of their time, it is evident that by reason of the consciousness they had of the fundamental importance of the choice of language they were to make, they too were creatively language-conscious. Though the Bible and Shakespeare have been the outstanding formative influences among writers of the English language, others too have made their contributions. Among these one very interesting and instructive class consists of those who have not only themselves used the language especially well, but have also made surveys, critical suggestions or creative experiments in linguistic usage. These are the formative working critics; and they extend from Chaucer to the present day.

Chaucer shewed himself a keen critic of poetic method and usage, but also a most interested student of language. In his *Reeve's Tale* he portrays two North-country undergraduates at Cambridge, using their native dialect when alone together. This is probably the first time that an English author shewed a conscious interest in dialect as opposed to the educated speech which was to become the received standard, and saw the possibilities of provincialism in speech as a source for humour and vividness. Chaucer also devoted a short humorous poem to the chastising of his scribe for his haste and negligence in copying his poems, and at the end of his greatest poem, *Troilus and Criseyde*, inserted a prayer for its correct copying and the avoidance of errors of metre or language:—

> And for ther is so greet diversitee
> In English and in wryting of our tonge,
> So preye I God that noon miswryte thee,
> Ne thee mismetre for defaute of tonge.
> And red wher-so thou be, or elles songe,
> That thou be understonde, I God beseche.'

It is often wrongly supposed that Chaucer had a dominant influence on the development of the English language. But, as has been seen, no writer, especially before the rise of printing, could have much effect on the language as a whole; and it was inevitable that the educated London speech which Chaucer happened to be born into should become the basis of the modern received standard. But in making much of the common poetic diction of Western Europe available in English, and through the dominant influence he exercised on the poets who followed him, Chaucer did much for the tradition of the language of English poetry. It is interesting to notice that in asking his contemporary Gower at the end of his *Troilus and Criseyde* to *correcte* his work, Chaucer was using the verb 'to correct' as a literary term three centuries before Dryden first introduced the corresponding adjective *correct* (from the French) into the language of literary criticism.

Spenser, in the later sixteenth century, beginning as a keen but romantic student of Chaucer, devoted his first considerable poem *The Shepheardes Calender* to linguistic experiment in great part. To prepare himself for finding the appropriate language for his 'lond of Faerie' in his *Faerie Queene*, he tried out various kinds of archaism in style, accidence and vocabulary. He also experimented with dialect-words found in earlier authors, with rustic provincial terms heard among his contemporaries, and even coined an occasional word. Nothing permanent came of all this, though his pastoral had its influence on English poetry for a time. But his *Faerie Queene* provided the language of poetry with *derring-do* (already coined in the *Shepheardes Calender*) and *faerie* itself, and the language of prose and ordinary speech (though with changed meaning) with *blatant*. Though only this word *blatant* may be said fully to have passed into the language as a whole, Spenser's *bragadochio* is still in literary use. But in the making of the language of romantic English poetry the *Faerie Queene* has had a considerable part. The Old French word *faerie* 'enchantment' or 'the place of enchantment', first appears in Middle English in a mixed Classical and Celtic romance called *Sir Orfeo* in which the classical harper Orpheus fetched home his wife Eurydice from a mysterious *Lond of Faerie* which was a mixture of the Celtic fairyland and the classical Hades: and Spenser took over this phrase *lond of Faerie* for his own poem, embellishing the word *faerie* with all kinds of new romantic connotations, so that it has become through his influence a specially productive word in later English poetry. This *faerie* with so much romantic poetic suggestiveness, has become through Spenser a separate term from the ordinary word *fairy* (of the same origin ultimately) which exists along with it. Spenser was, then, by implication, a working critic of the language whose labours were productive in diction for the succeeding poetry.

Dryden, to turn now to a writer of far wider scope

than Spenser, wrote every kind of literature, in prose as well as verse, which his age seemed to ask for; he was also in many an essay, prologue and preface, a literary critic who discussed the questions of language as they presented themselves. He regarded himself, as may be seen from his private letters, as a conscious improver of the language. He was a member of the Royal Society's committee on English, and had the project of an English academy which might do for the language something like what the *Académie Française* was doing for French. He suffered like most writers of his day, from the notion that the language was or could be static, thinking that of his own age superior to what had gone before and as good as it could be. He often changed his mind and was inconsistent in his linguistic judgements. But, apart from his work for the improvement of the metre and diction of English poetry, one thing stands out as of particular interest: his aim to bring the language of poetry nearer to that of conversation, as well as to improve prose in the same direction. He was one of the first to discuss the language of his predecessors, including Shakespeare. It cannot be said that he added much of note to the English vocabulary. But his interest in all phases of language made him a pioneer; and at least his efforts to make poetry more conversational were of formative significance, and have influenced poets as lately as Mr. T. S. Eliot. His more colloquial prose too, with its deliberate seeking after clarity and simplicity, had its influence.

A very different working critic was **Dr. Johnson**: for he had scholarship and method in his work for the language far beyond those of **Dryden**, though he was

not often a poet. Of his *Dictionary*, with its fundamental influences, we have already spoken. To it he
prefixed an account of English grammar and of the
language, which still has value. He liked a language of
firm tradition and disliked change: yet he came late
in life to realize fully the inevitably changing nature
of language, as Dryden never did. Almost always, in
writing his *Lives of the Poets*, he included some criticism of the poet's language, and often added to these
comments his own general linguistic views. He was
the first to set out clearly, in his *Proposals for editing
Shakespeare* and in the Preface to his edition, the
principles of Shakespearean textual criticism; and in
so doing he applied a keen knowledge of the language
over a wide range of authors. It has often wrongly
been said that Johnson greatly Latinized his language
in style and vocabulary. The truth is rather that he
frequently modelled his prose on that of his favourite
seventeenth-century writers such as Sir Thomas
Browne. Such writers, in a learned age, used many
words of Latin origin which have not survived in
common usage, and they sought balance and rhythm
in their English with the aid of Latin prose-style and
the sonority of Latinate words judiciously employed.
Johnson did this too, and in his less mature work
with exaggeration. But he very seldom coined a word
from Latin, and has scarcely added anything to the
English vocabulary. Yet as a critic of the language,
as a dominantly influential lexicographer and as a
maker of prose that was formative for others, he was
supreme for his time.

Chaucer, Spenser, Dryden and Dr. Johnson, have
been chosen for mention as great and formative
representative working critics of the language. The

list of such authors could, of course, be made very long. Milton, however, who could equally well be placed in this category or among the great formative poets, is important enough to merit separate treatment.

5. MILTON AND THE ENGLISH LANGUAGE

Apart from the outstanding position of Milton as a moulder and exemplar of English poetic diction, which does not directly concern us here, he is of interest in at least three ways to the student of the development of the English language. He had ideas on spelling, with which he experimented; he was a keen student of the language and a supreme practitioner in it; and he has added a number of words and phrases to the literary vocabulary if not to the spoken.

Milton was the last great poet who deliberately composed verses to be recited or read *aloud*, rather than merely read: and his blindness probably made him especially conscious of the importance of emphasis and pronunciation when causing his amanuensis to write down his *Paradise Lost* for the printer. Though in no sense a 'spelling-reformer', he was keenly concerned in spelling in his later life for aesthetic reasons. The MS. of the First Book of *Paradise Lost* prepared under his dictation, is extant, as are also the notes of errors made by the first printer in sometimes failing to carry out Milton's instructions in the matter of orthography. From this evidence it is clear that he tried to indicate a distinction in spelling, for instance, between the stressed and the unstressed forms of the personal pronouns—

mee, hee, shee and *their* for the emphatic forms, and *me, he, she* and *thir* for the weaker ones. He took measures to ensure that the reader aloud should know by the spelling whether the ending of weak past participles in *-d* was to be pronounced as a separate syllable *-ed* or not; and he also insisted on ending such words with a *-t* rather than a *-d* whenever the natural pronunciation suggested it (*walkt* for 'walked'). Where the contemporary habits provided a choice of spelling in words that he had probably noticed as liable to mispronunciation, Milton preferred the form nearest to the actual sound —*sovran* for *sovereign* and *artic* for *arctic*, with *island* without the *s* as *iland*. He shewed his sensitiveness to pronunciation and interest in what we now call phonetics by seeking to indicate the syllabic *-n* as distinct from the sound *-en* by writing *heaven* and *forbidden* as *heav'n* and *forbidd'n* when he required the last syllable to be slurred and consonantal as against the fuller forms with vowel+consonant. Indeed he even made his scribe cross out the *e* of *forbidden* and substitute an apostrophe for this reason in the second line of the poem:—

'Of that forbidd'n Tree whose mortall tast'.

Milton had no influence on English spelling (except on the recent poet Robert Bridges): nor did his printers at all exactly carry out his ideas: and these ideas were not consistently or thoroughly worked out. Yet this sensitiveness to pronunciation in a poet like Milton, who was also one of the most exact rhymers, is of interest in itself.

At the age of nineteen, Milton employed the English part of a vacation exercise at Cambridge to

proclaim his attitude to the vernacular, in the
following words:—

> 'Hail native Language, that by sinews weak
> Didst move my first endeavouring tongue to speak,
>
> .   .   .   .   .
>
> And from thy wardrobe bring thy chiefest treasure;
> Not those new fangled toys, and triming slight
> Which takes our late fantasticks with delight,
> But cull those richest Robes, and gay'st attire
> Which deepest Spirits, and choicest Wits desire:
>
> .   .   .   .   .
>
> Yet I had rather if I were to chuse,
> Thy service in some graver subject use,
> *Such as may make thee search thy coffers round,*
> *Before thou cloath my fancy in fit sound.*'

In a learned age when Latin was still the language of
philosophy and science, Milton, in the midst of the
Latin discipline of Cambridge, voices his preoccupa-
tion with the possibilities of the native language, and
proclaims his faith in English as having potentially
all the qualities needed for the highest poetry. From
that time Milton was studying to make himself such
a master of English that he could make the utmost
use of all its capacities, could 'make thee search thy
coffers round'. Here he shews himself a critic of the
linguistic usages of some of his contemporary poets,
the 'late fantasticks': and there are, in his prose
pamphlets as well as in his poems, occasional critical
utterances on questions of language. For example,
his note entitled *The Verse*, prefixed to *Paradise Lost*,
touches the question of music in language. Though
its insistence on 'fit quantity of syllables' shews a
confusion between stress (emphasis) and quantity
(duration), this passage indicates one aspect of a keen
linguistic conscience.

Milton's English has often been objected to as

extremely Latinate. But most of the supposed Latinizing in the vocabulary of his later work turns out, on examination with the aid of the *New English Dictionary*, to be only the deliberate use for selected effect of words of Latin origin now obsolete but already familiar among the best educated in the learned seventeenth century who were to form his 'fit audience', 'though few'. It is rather in the matter of syntax that Milton shews how closely he has been influenced by the models of Latin prose then familiar. Often the syntax is not fully intelligible to anyone not conversant with the Latin constructions which are reproduced in English. Yet what puzzles or strikes as unnatural in Milton's occasionally extremely Latin syntax, would have seemed much more natural and appropriate to his contemporaries. Milton was, after Shakespeare, the greatest master in English poetic language, though more limited in the ground he covered: but this is not the place to enlarge on his poetic making of English to suit the 'grand style'. But besides being the master in poetic diction of so many who have followed, Milton has left some notable marks on the language which go far beyond this sphere.

The now common word *pandemonium* was first coined by Milton to describe the palace built in Hell by the devils, from the Greek *pan* 'all' and *daimōn* 'devil'. Like Spenser's *blatant,* this word has become commonplace in speech as well as in writing, but with a loosened and debased sense. Milton's dignified and classically built palace of *pandæmonium* (*Paradise Lost*, I, 756) is now in colloquial speech little more than 'the hell of a row'! In *Paradise Lost* are found Milton's phrases which, taken from their contexts, have become familiar in all kinds of extended uses in the language. Here are some of them:— *precious bane* for 'gold' (I, 692), *from noon to dewy eve* (I, 743), *secret conclave* (I, 795), *the gorgeous East* (II, 3), *prove a bitter morsel* (II, 808), *confusion worse confounded* (II, 996), *hide thir diminisht heads* (IV, 35), *a heaven on earth* (IV, 208), *wild work in heav'n* (VI, 698), *to save appearances* (VIII, 82), and *a pillar of state* (II, 302). These are only the more widely used of Milton's phrases: many more occur in purely literary language.

The occasional use of dialect-words and archaism for special effects, Milton practised like the Elizabethans whom he knew well. His early poems shew a good deal of the influence of Spenser's *Faerie Queene* and of his kind of archaism. Mention has been made earlier of his use of the provincial term *charm* (*Paradise Lost*, IV, 642) for the song of birds with almost magical effect in suggesting rusticity: but he had tried out this word, so to speak, in the line from *Il Penseroso* (83)

> 'Or the Belmans drousie charm.'

In *Lycidas* (124) he had used the probably Lincolnshire word of Norse origin *scrannel* 'harsh and thin' similarly for its effect in its context: of some contemporary pastoral lyric poets he says

> 'And when they list, their lean and flashy songs
> Grate on their *scrannel* Pipes of wretched straw.'

Following a poem in the collection called *England's Helicon* published in 1600, he used the properly gardening term *rathe* 'quickly maturing' in the line in the same poem (142):

> 'Bring the rathe Primrose that forsaken dies.'

Here the latter part of the line echoes a Shakespearean idea. In *Comus* (312) he brought into literary use the West-country term *dingle*, which had only been recorded in Drayton since the beginning of the thirteenth century outside of place-names.

Shakespeare and the Bible were perhaps the greatest English influences upon Milton's language. The multitude of imitations of Latin and occasionally even Greek constructions and poetic phrases, has tended to obscure his extraordinary variety and breadth of culture in using the English resources of the language. He did not often coin a word; and apart from *pandemonium* which has become part of the language outside of literature, there are only purely literary words such as *anarch* (*Paradise Lost*, II, 988), which he made from Greek to express the peculiar attributes of his Chaos. The deliberate use of simple words for special effect in the midst of a rhythmic Latinized diction, he practised often most effectively: for he was a master of the plainest English diction as well as of his grand poetic style designed for the sublime matters of his *Paradise Lost*. Like the Bible translations and Shakespeare, his more outstanding permanent influence on the English language is to be seen in his phrases; and these too are still widely used among those who have never looked into Milton's writings.

6. SOME POETS AND THE LANGUAGE

Of the poets not already touched upon, Pope and Wordsworth have been, for very different reasons, the most influential on the language as a whole: and it must be remembered that we are concerned in this chapter primarily with those who have left their impression on the English language in general, and not with the special merits of the language of the authors in itself.

Pope is pre-eminently the poet who has given us in elegant and memorable form, as he puts it,

> 'Nature to advantage drest,
> What oft was thought, but ne'er so well expressed.'

Several of his neat expressions of obvious truths have passed into the language far beyond the readers of poetry. Such are 'A little learning is a dangerous thing'; 'Hope springs eternal in the human breast'; and 'Damn with faint praise'. Milton and the Latin classical poets were often his sources of inspiration; but he had a genius for the *mot juste* for the commonly acceptable idea. He could write in the familiar conversational style too when he liked. His influence on poets has been very considerable. His avowed aiming at 'correctness' in poetic language too had a good disciplining effect.

Wordsworth thought himself a pioneer in seeking to write poetry in 'a selection of the language really used by men'. He sought to bring the vocabulary of poetry into the language of actual speech of a simple and dignified kind, holding, at least in his earlier life, that 'There is no *essential* difference between the language of prose and that of metrical composition.' In this he was in some measure continuing a tradition of familiar language in certain kinds of verse, which had existed at least since the twelfth century, and in which Chaucer had excelled. But shocked by the 'false poetic diction' of much of the eighteenth century, he tried to preach and to practise in early life the theory that such differences as undoubtedly existed between the language of verse and prose were inessential, and that a more or less common vocabulary was possible. He did not know of the Anglo-Saxon and Middle English alliterative poetry, whose diction is utterly remote from that of prose and yet was a valued tradition to its audiences: nor, on the other hand, had he noticed sufficiently the conversational style of much later verse. But he went further, and for some time believed that in the language of rustics was to be found the right medium for poetry. For he believed that such people 'hourly communicate with the best objects, from which the best part of language is originally derived'. He had no understanding of the fact that the vivid and strong parts of the vocabulary of the rustic are just those which are the most dialectal, the local names for the acts and things of his own daily life—whereas for 'the best parts of nature' he usually has no detailed vocabulary. Wordsworth did not realize how varied were the dialects spoken in the England of his time, in which, for instance, the speech of the Cumberland dalesmen was unintelligible to men of London. Nor did he understand the immense value of poetic tradition in language, though himself steeped in the deepest influences from Shakespeare and Milton. He also does not seem to have grasped the point that, even though poetry and prose may use the same vocabulary, the metaphorical and other uses of the same words is likely to differ in the two media. He could write simply and well when the situation and context favoured this, as in his poem *Michael*. He could write with unnatural and conscious simplicity, and badly when thinking on his theories of diction. In all his best work, however, he is clearly following.

in the matter of choice of language, in the steps of the best poets who wrote before him, and using the instinct produced by that training in diction. One of his best 'simple poems' is the following on *Lucy*:

> 'A slumber did my spirit seal;
> I had no human fears;
> She seemed a thing that could not feel
> The touch of earthly years.
> No motion has she now, no force:
> She neither hears nor sees—
> Roll'd round in earth's diurnal course,
> With rocks and stones and trees.'

Here the word *seal* in the first line is used in an un-proselike metaphorical sense, and *slumber* is not a word of homely speech. In the last two lines there is a general echo in the tone from Milton's *Paradise Lost*, and the use of *diurnal* here must have come unconsciously from the deep assimilation of Milton. Wordsworth has been an influence on poetic language in general: but he scarcely ever used a real dialect-word (*by-spots* being the one clear example), and has not brought any special contribution to the English vocabulary. Yet, as with any great poet, some of his phrases have remained in the literary language at least, such as 'The still sad music of humanity'. Towards a homely diction the Dorset poet William Barnes, who was also a considerable amateur philologist, worked by means of adapting the dialect of his county to poetry, as Wordsworth had never thought of doing; and others have followed with varying knowledge and success. But it can scarcely be said that any great dialect poetry has yet been produced; and the 'dialect' of verse is more often of a romantic than an exact type.

This use of dialect as an experiment may be considered as part of an increasing dissatisfaction with the traditional resources of language and attempts to adjust the English language to the rapidly changing and far more complex mental processes of the modern world. Experiments have lately been made in the language, especially of verse and of 'prose-poetry', comparable with the efforts of surrealist painters. Spelling, typography, technical and occupational regions of vocabulary, the supposed language of the subconscious mind, symbolism, impressionism, and much else have been called in to make the poets' language more expressive. But few of such experiments appear to have yet accomplished any clear good result, and more recently there has been some marked looking back to the more traditional and easily understood usages of the language. As typical, yet intensely individual and of real poetic ability among these experimenters, we may take the later nineteenth-century pioneer in linguistic exploring, Gerard Manley Hopkins, whose work did not become known to the public generally till Robert Bridges published a volume of it in 1918.

Like Milton, G. M. Hopkins had studied both the Classical sources of English literature and the English writings that had most contributed to the development of the language: and like him he sought—in the very limited time he could give to such matters—to

> 'Make thee search thy coffers round
> Until thou clothe my fancy in fit sound.'

With a wide knowledge of the older poetry and of something of the technicalities of its language, he taxed the resources of English to their utmost, indeed sometimes seeming to be fain to invent a new kind of English, with new words, revivals and new-made compounds to express his so intense and so individual consciousness of natural beauty as the expression of spiritual fact. The Elizabethans, as we have noticed particularly in discussing Shakespeare, were very fertile in reviving and increasing the old gift of the English language for the making and the enlarging of its capacity for forming compounds: and imitations of Greek compounds found in Homer, like Spenser's 'Rosy-finger'd' (Homer's *Rhododaktylos*) as an epithet for the dawn, had also had some successes at that time. Very shortly afterwards Donne had made a minor revolutionary effort in verse by combining a very colloquial turn of language with the use of technical terms from recent science and from mediaeval philosophy and theology. This blend of the colloquial and the technical in a freer conception of poetic rhythm, which often characterized Donne and which has appealed to so many poets in the years following the war of 1914–18, is markedly shewn in Hopkins as well as this freer compounding: and it is probable that his influence and example have had considerable effect, however temporarily, on the language of English poetry. His experimenting with astonishing compounds and new arrangements of words is often combined with the employment of all kinds of technical terms, colloquial idiom and linguistic echoes from the Schools and religious seminaries. But he also found it necessary to have new and specialized terms for his own aesthetic and thought-processes, such as *instress*, *inscape* and *love-scape*. Like Mr. Auden in his earlier verse, he sometimes used archaism along with new modes of expression or new rhythms. He

sought to revive and extend older devices of poetry
such as alliteration and purely accentual rhythm, in
so intimate a union with his partially new kind of
language in all its tense individualism, so as almost
to create a new medium of expression, requiring wide
knowledge and concentration for its understanding.
Here is probably the simplest and least eccentric
poem he wrote, yet it is markedly individual, experimental and difficult in language:

Pied Beauty
'Glory be to God for dappled things—
For skies of couple-colour as a brinded cow;
For rose-moles all in stipple upon trout that swim;
Fresh-firecoal chestnut-falls; finches' wings;
Landscape plotted and pieced—fold, fallow, and plough;
And áll trádes, their gear and tackle and trim.
All things counter, original, spare, strange;
Whatever is fickle, freckled (who knows how?)
With swift, slow; sweet, sour; adazzle, dim;
He fathers-forth whose beauty is past change:
Praise him.'

This is characteristic; but commonly Hopkins's verses
are far more removed from traditional language or
contemporary speech than this. It is not that he has
influenced the language, but rather that he shews
markedly tendencies in his use and arrangement of
words which were typical of poetry that followed
him. He represents, in a small corner of the field,
tendencies in recent literary English, although, as has
been said, the latest writing in verse suggests a looking back to more traditional and easily understood
methods. The extreme in seeking to make language
express the subconscious and symbolize impressions
without saying anything intelligible in detail (unless
with the aid of technical explanations) is reached in

the later writings of James Joyce, and commentators have not yet managed to make much of his *Finnegans Wake* mean anything to many. It is too soon to estimate what this perhaps ephemeral episode in the history of the literary language may mean. From two notable periods of keen linguistic interest and experimental dissatisfaction with things as they were in language, the Elizabethan and the time of passing from the eighteenth to the nineteenth centuries (the 'Romantic revival' period) many good developments followed: and this too may turn out to be such a time of experimentation preceding new and valuable growths. Certain it is that, both among writers and professional philosophers, there has been of late a marked interest in the nature and the potentialities of language, and a re-awakened curiosity.

7. RHETORIC AND ORATORY

To-day, though vaster crowds than ever before can be addressed by an orator, the numbers of those who in fact listen to public speeches are less than formerly by a good deal. The wireless too is the medium of far more frequent verbal communication than any kind of orator. Education has tended lately to cover a less wide and ample field of that kind of knowledge which makes for effective allusions and thought-tickling wit. That leisurely acquisition of knowledge along with aesthetic growth and mental alertness, which is a necessary preparation for the kind of oratory we admire in Burke, the younger Pitt or Mr. Churchill, is no longer often to be come by. Similarly rhetorical writing of good literary quality that might have lasting influence, is now rarely to be met with. Social

conditions militate against the production of the good
speaker or the literary rhetorician. But in the past
the language has owed something to great speakers,
and to those who have used the rhetorical method in
writing like Macaulay or Ruskin.

No orator or rhetorical writer has had any marked
influence on the language as a whole that can be
demonstrated, in the same sense in which Shakespeare
or the Bible, or even Dr. Johnson, have influenced it.
But great speakers and writers of rhetorical prose
have left examples which have had their effect on the
general development of the language; and occasionally
the phrases, allusions or tricks of style of such persons
have become part of English. Amid the abundant
Common European clichés and stereotyped phrases
which may now be read or heard in almost all the
tongues of Europe, Mr. Churchill's best speeches
stand out for their apt literary allusions and the
rhythm and balance of the prose, for their suggestion
of a strong and individual personality and familiarity
with so many of the varied resources of the English
language. But from the point of view of English
linguistic history, it seems likely that his demon-
strable permanent contribution to the language will
be found to consist in the influence of his example
and in some vivid and memorable phrases, like his
'dusty answer' (echoed from Meredith), 'blood, toil,
tears and sweat', and in sentences of simple con-
centrated force which say 'what oft was thought
but ne'er so well expressed' like his 'Never was so
much owed by so many to so few'. From the eighteenth and nineteenth centuries, which were the
great ages of Parliamentary oratory, Burke's
written speeches (for it seems that his delivery

was not such as to hold an audience with anything like the same power as that which still enchants and stimulates the readers of his orations) stand out as supreme. Besides furnishing models for endless imitation, they have given a few phrases to the literary language. He used to the utmost all the resources of the language, including its greatest masters. The Authorized Version of the Bible, Shakespeare and Milton his speeches shew him thoroughly to have assimilated; and he knew Dryden and Pope well. He had, like Mr. Churchill, always an amazing individuality, a most telling literary allusiveness and the gift to use the simplest words when appropriate in the midst of high flights of rhetoric. But though the linguistic influence of his work is to be seen far and wide in the English-educated natives of what was formerly the British Empire, in England now his speeches are only read, for the most part, by the professional student. Yet in simple rhetorical sayings like his 'The age of chivalry is gone', he is still unconsciously occasionally echoed.

CHAPTER VII

THE ENGLISH LANGUAGE TO-DAY

I. GENERAL CONSIDERATIONS

WE have now sketched the broad outline of the history of English. We have seen the growth and the sources of its vocabulary, and something of the historical relationship between its spelling and its pronunciation. We have looked into the shaping and arranging of its words and the development of their ever-changing meanings; and we have glanced back at the work of some of its outstanding masters who have used its full resources well and done something to mould its future. We ought, therefore, to be now in a position to take a clearer view of the English language to-day. Yet we can scarcely expect even now to attain to that objectiveness which it is fashionable to seek, in viewing the English of to-day. For we ourselves are among the users—and therefore the makers, of this ever-moving and growing organism: and the actor on the linguistic stage is not a likely person to be able to estimate the qualities of the medium he is himself using. Moreover, English is now well on the way to becoming a world-language: and this means many types of English, many pronunciations and vocabulary-groups within the English language. There is, for instance, an Indian—and even a Bengali form of English which is yet to at least some extent a living language. Then again, while our knowledge of the past history of the language should help us in the understanding of many things in it to-day, it is also true that the feeling for linguistic tradition thus engendered is likely at times to prejudice our exactness in observing and assessing its present qualities and tendencies. But though we may not, therefore, be able to pass judgement on the English of to-day, we can to some extent notice the outstanding tendencies it is shewing. We can see the obvious influence upon it of American speech, the growth of new types of slang such as that of the cinema, the effects at times of broadcasting on pronunciation, and the increased freedom or, as some would say, looseness in using the language. We can notice the effects of the many changes in social life on speech, and the linguistic results, it may be, of the widening of school education and the reduced influence of a more traditional and Classical education which had been a brake upon change and a conserver of usage. We can note the vast effects of widespread and universally accessible printing and of journalism, and many other features which seem fairly well evidenced. But all this is only material for a descriptive survey. To attempt to assess the value of these tendencies or the probable future of the language is fascinating, but necessarily only hypothetic and speculative. Without an established linguistic scale of values, such judgements can have no certainty and are best left to each individual to make for himself. But the desire for a 'standard' of English and a growing self-consciousness in matters of language, is itself one of the tendencies to be noticed: and the question 'What is correct' in speech or writing becomes more and more frequent among all kinds of people.

This chapter will attempt to indicate some of the

marked tendencies of the English of to-day, but will not venture—for the reasons already mentioned—to pronounce judgement or to prophesy.

2. THE SEARCH FOR A STANDARD

It is natural that, in an age of some psychological advance and much consequent superficial talk and writing about psychology, there should be a growth of self-consciousness in linguistic usage, side by side with the growth of a more introspective mental habit. Hence perhaps the increased seeking after 'correctness' in English and the looking after a 'received standard'. Yet just in so far as a speaker becomes exactly conscious of the sounds of his speech, that speech will become less natural—less truly the expression of his own personality. Let the reader try for himself the experiment of listening to his own voice while making a speech, and the truth of this statement will become clear.

Then, from another point of view, it may be asked, what do we look for in a 'correct' or 'good' type of English? Is the main criterion to be aesthetic or practical? Do we prefer the English whose sound pleases our ear, or that which is clearest and most intelligible? And if we decide to support that which pleases for its beauty of sound or elegance of form, is there anything like a generally accepted standard of beauty? No doubt the emphasis should in large measure depend on the particular purpose for which the language is to be employed. Broadcasters, for instance, seek a type of English which combines the maximum of clearness and intelligibility with the minimum of shock. That is, they strive to be well

heard over the widest area and to be understood; but
at the same time to avoid as far as possible pronunciations or usages that are likely to shock or surprise any
part of their audience. An orator, on the other hand,
may be expected to seek beauty in his language,
and qualities to stir up an emotional response,
along with the gifts of the broadcaster mentioned
above.

'Good English' may be described as the English of
the educated classes used without self-consciousness.
For educated people would have the good traditions
of the language well assimilated, would have enough
development of their personality to use the resources
of the language fully, and would have enough discipline to avoid vagueness and jargon or clichés.
Such people might also be expected to use that relatively uniform pronunciation which is becoming
current generally, with sensitiveness of ear which
would prevent sounds and usages ugly or harsh to
the majority. But this is only a very rough statement. It must also be remembered that we can only
speak of a 'received standard English' when referring
to the educated language of England, as far as pronunciation is concerned. There are many types of
'good English' as described above outside of England
—that of Edinburgh in Scotland, for example, or
that of Philadelphia or Boston in America. In the
written language, however, there is relative uniformity among the more educated users of English the
whole world over. The answer, then, to the question
'What is correct', is 'what educated speakers say',
not what they ought—according to some notions of
grammar or dictionary—to say.

Broadly speaking, it may be said there are three

types of spoken English in England: 'received standard', regional dialects, and 'modified standard'. 'Received standard' is good English in the sense already indicated. Regional dialects are those of localized use in rural areas where a fairly uniform and immobile community still predominates, such as those of Cumberland or South Devon. 'Modified standard' (an expression used by the late H. C. Wyld) is the speech of that large number of people who have been bred in a regional or occupational dialect, have 'corrected' this in schools and colleges, but have not succeeded in reaching to more than some half-way house between a local dialect and the standard English aimed at. This modified standard has limitless varieties and shades. To these three types of English might be added the always mixed or heterogeneous speech of large industrial towns where the population is mobile and from varied localities; and many dialects have influenced one another and become blurred and blended into a common speech. There are, too, small occupational dialects, such as that of Yorkshire West Riding textile-workers, which have their own specialized vocabulary within a regional dialect.

While, on the one hand, the needs of modern life require a universally clear and comprehensible form of English and therefore suggest a received standard of pronunciation to be learned and used by all, there is nothing necessarily superior in this 'good English' as against regional dialects. For a rural dialect may contain vivid and even delicate shades of expression, phrases or words, that are unequalled in the standard language: and a speaker to whom a regional dialect is natural, will not fully express his mind in a merely acquired type of speech. Nor is exact uniformity of pronunciation to be aimed at, even if it were possible. For it is for the sake of being universally understood that we should cultivate a generally received kind of English: but within that requirement there is a good deal of room for variety of dialect-produced pronunciation and intonation. Indeed to many the 'correct' pronunciation of professional broadcasters may sound flat and lifeless, lacking colour and musical quality.

3. AMERICAN INFLUENCE

English and the speech of the United States are one language: but in the more than three centuries that have passed since the first settlements, each has developed in divergent ways—both in its generally accepted 'standard' forms and in dialects. While it will be obvious to anyone that American speech and written language have developed new elements—in vocabulary, phrasing, structure and pronunciation—it is not so well known that many older usages of English have been preserved in America which have disappeared from Britain. There are in American use, archaisms such as the preservation of *gotten* as the past participle of *get*, *fall* for 'autumn', *aim to* for the later English use of *aim at*, and *faucet* for *tap*. Many seventeenth-century usages have survived in standard American, and far more in some of the dialects: and some of these, like *fall* for 'autumn', may well seem more attractive than their English equivalents. American has developed new ways of speech, partly through differing conditions of life, partly through its having received many influences from other languages in the process of its absorption of large bodies of immigrants from many lands. The primary difference between English and American is in the rhythm and intonation of speech: but there are many differences in shade of meaning in the common shared stock of English vocabulary, as well as new words and new metaphorical usages found first in America and only now beginning to take root in Britain. For example, *politician* has a disparaging sense in America which it does not yet carry in England; *solicitor* means a canvasser or visiting agent or beggar in America; and *clerk* more often means a shop-assistant than anyone else.

The English of educated standard American, then, is just as much a 'good English' as that of educated London: but the 'clipped syllables' which the American hears in Englishmen's pronunciation as against the 'drawl' and 'nasal tone' which the Englishman notices in American, are in reality differences in rhythm and intonation which shew the development of two types of English. Such differences are enhanced by changes of meaning in the same words, new words in both forms of English, etc. But it is too soon to say whether these divergent developments will later produce two distinct languages, whether they will draw nearer together with the increased freedom of intercourse, or whether (as some Americans incline to think) American English will absorb that of Britain. Each has its formal and its slovenly types of speech, as each has its archaic and its rapidly changing features.

It is, however, certain that American English has very considerably influenced British English—especially in the last quarter of a century: and this has been due to a far wider set of circumstances than the mere fact of America's leading position in commerce, the films and finance—though these have produced a body of slang in England some of which has already penetrated to good colloquial usage. The word *caucus*, for instance, came to England as a political term from America, and has now developed a slightly different meaning. The use of *cut* as a word for 'reduction' was originally American, but became fixed in good English largely through the financial slump of 1931 in Britain and its consequences. *Sense* as a verb, which has been in use in the British written language for nearly a century, was an importation from America, and even to-day is frowned upon as a poor substitute for *perceive* or *feel* by some old-fashioned scholars.

But by far the most marked American influence-- and one which still seems to be increasing—is in the slang of the younger generation in Britain and in the colloquial English which springs from a selection of this. The films, naturally, are a prolific source of this kind of language: but one cannot guess how much of it may turn out to be only a passing fashion of speech. Vividness and force in metaphorical expression are characteristic of much American English; and it is natural, therefore, that a selection of these should be taken up into spoken English, especially by the young who are most eager for new linguistic experience. But there are metaphors from America far older than the cinema which are now part of colloquial good English, such as the phrase *to get down to brass tacks*. Among colloquial expressions in English from America may be mentioned the use of the verb *to fix* for a far wider number of senses than is current in written English or was known before the American influence, such as 'I'll fix it for you', or 'Try and fix it so that he escapes'. Again, at least in newspapers and commercial works, the word *executive* has become a noun in English under American influences, as in 'business *executives* are very highly paid'. No one is conscious now in Britain of using an American expression when speaking of *the party machine*; yet this was till lately a purely American use of *machine*.

Among slang expressions which have not yet—and may never—reach the good colloquial stage, are *dumb* for 'stupid', *frame-up* for 'trumped-up charge', *blue* 'depressed', *pass out* 'die' or 'faint', *O.K.* 'all right', and the noun *pull* in the sense of special individual influence (though this last may be thought by some already to have reached good colloquial status). The horde of slang terms from the film industry and from American 'gangster' and low life (real or supposed), needs no recording here.

In some ways it will appear that the recent American influence has done something to revitalize and invigorate British English—especially in vivid metaphor. On the other hand, vivid expressions if used as mere stereotyped phrases, when they were intended first in America for occasions of special emphasis and strength of language, may seem an impoverishment rather than an enrichment of speech. Perhaps it is in the language of British journalism of the more popular newspaper variety, that this superfluous use of American expressions where British English was already well provided with appropriate words, shews the weakness or the disadvantage of the cheaper American influences and is most to be deplored. But journalism is a special profession which has been practised on a far vaster scale in the United States than anywhere else in the world. It is significant that Mr. Churchill, with his talent for simple beauty of phrase, has shewn at one and the same time the influence of American English and of Shakespeare by beginning a speech with the words 'Before the fall of the autumn leaves'.

4. THE RADIO AND THE LANGUAGE

Until a quarter of a century ago, printing was the one means of broadcasting language, of making it as far as possible universally accessible. The spreading of English influence in many parts of the world, the coming of the cheap newspaper press, the making of education compulsory through the printed word with the fixation of the form and spelling of English through printing—all these and many other causes may seem to have been at work in the last centuries —especially since the coming of obligatory schooling in 1870—to standardize English in general, and to eliminate or confuse its dialects. Social and class dialects have come to replace or blur those based on region: but these too are subject to the standardizing influence of printing. It might seem, therefore, that the written word is on the way to becoming acceptable wherever English is used in recognized conventional dress, and that the language can now be observed from dictionaries with accuracy. A speaker of Canadian, or Australian English, for example, of the cultured type, is using almost exactly the same *written* form of English, though their speech differs a good deal in pronunciation, rhythm and intonation.

But, as has been said by the editors of the *Oxford English Dictionary*, 'The pronunciation is the actual living form or forms of a word, that is, *the word itself*,

of which the current spelling is only a symbolization.'
Whatever conventions of spelling may seem to be
fixed, the spoken word must, by the very nature of
language, continue to change. It is questionable
whether, with the use of English in so many different
pronunciations among so many utterly diverse peoples
all over the world, the forces of the standardized
written language will be strong enough to resist the
tendencies to disintegration and fragmentation which
the world-wide use of English in hundreds of pronunciations and local types of spoken idiom, must bring.
Can an English so variously pronounced, spoken with
such heterogeneousness of non-English native idioms
and interlarded with so many local elements, be kept
from disintegration and loss of unity as a language by
the power of printing and all that that implies?

The setting up in London of the official broadcasting centre in 1922, and the rapid developments from
this comparatively small beginning, suggest that
there is now a second aid to the conservation of 'good
English'. Side by side with printing, the radio must
now be recognized as a second means of making the
language universally accessible. But further, the
standardizing and conservative tendencies provided
by official broadcasting may help to check the disintegration of the spoken language, and even to encourage a far more uniform type by means of the
influence of trained and directed announcers. Can
the spoken broadcast word do for the real language of
speakers, what the printed word has done for that of
writers? How far, in fact, are ordinary people influenced by the kind of English they listen to from
the British Broadcasting Corporation? Now that the
voices of the B.B.C. are heard in specially prepared

cadences and usages all over the world by people who do not speak the language at home or only in a distinctively local pronunciation, will Broadcasting House and its offshoots set up a recognized standard of spoken English in some measure comparable to that set up for the written language in printing?

In 1926 the B.B.C., finding some of its speakers in difficulty over words of doubtful pronunciation—especially place-names and foreign names—set up an *Advisory Committee on Spoken English*: and this later developed from small beginnings to the issuing of pamphlets to the general public of decisions and advice on special points of pronunciation originally intended only for the guidance of official announcers. In issuing its views on pronunciation, the B.B.C. seemed to some to be using its Advisory Committee on Spoken English somewhat like the nucleus of some sort of Academy analogous to the *Académie Française*: and this impression might seem to be strengthened by the multitude of English lessons of all kinds broadcast all over the world from London. The B.B.C. never made any such claim—and indeed has always insisted that it had no such intention. But naturally some of the less well-informed among the public have tended to regard the radio announcer as having in some sort the voice of authority. In a number of English words there have long been equally acceptable or 'correct' alternative pronunciations: for good English includes a good deal of variety of pronunciation within itself. On the other hand, there are many Northern educated speakers, for instance, who feel that the definitely Southern pronunciation of standard English adopted by the B.B.C. is less pleasing, or even less natural, than their own. If it were merely a matter of counting heads, too, it seems likely that the Northern and North Midland pronunciation of a more raised and fronted vowel in words like *fast* and *ask*, should be preferred as being more representative of English as a whole. Then again, the more 'expert' academic side of the Advisory Committee on Spoken English tended to count for less as against the influence of distinguished members from the non-academic public: and it has sometimes happened that pronunciations accepted by the B.B.C. have been later rejected by those apparently well qualified to judge. To counterbalance this danger, the B.B.C. has issued provisional decisions on points of pronunciation, and then re-considered these in the light of criticism received from the public. But it is doubtful if a majority decision on such matters is necessarily the right one.

In recognizing by its Regional divisions of programme, such as those of Wales and Scotland, that there are good types of English in various areas, the B.B.C. has been realistic.

It is too soon, in the quarter of a century during which the B.B.C. has been active, to determine in anything more than conjecture, how far the influence of its standardizing tendencies for spoken English are likely to have large or lasting results. But it is clear that at least in parts of the world where English is spoken other than as the Mother Tongue, the constant hearing of a conventionalized form of the language is likely to serve as a conserving model, and in so far to form something of an obstacle to the disintegration of the language as speech. Another fact of the recent development in the approach to English which may reasonably be in part ascribed to the influence of broadcasting, is the growing interest in the nature of speech, in the need for clear and pleasing utterance and the ability to express one's thoughts in effective language. There are societies for the training of speech, special academic studies in the diseases and disabilities of speakers and their cure (speech-therapy), increased study of phonetics in universities and some schools, the keen interest in the reciting of poetry, and the special attention now encouraged by many authorities on education to the teaching of good habits of speech to children as well as adults. The dangers of mere linguistic self-consciousness have already been touched upon: but there can be no doubt that increased interest in good speaking is an immense gain. For the bringing of this growing interest to good fruit, the study of the language *as a whole*—both its past, and the present state which can only be fully understood from a knowledge of that past—is most especially to be desired.

It must be remembered in all these matters, that language is a natural growth, and therefore should not be forced. Good English must be clear, seem natural to the hearer, and an effective expression of the speaker's thoughts. The use of the English language to its full capacity is an ideal. But while self-consciousness will prevent naturalness and vividness of expression, the training of a sensitive ear and the development of a faculty for linguistic observation are likely to promote this end. 'Proper words in proper places', as Swift said, is a description of good style; and this is true of speech as much as of writing. To the accuracy and sensitive imitation of the best, which speech-training may produce, that deeper feeling for the language and understanding of its potentialities which the good speaker needs, can only be added by knowledge. That is one of the chief reasons for the study of the history of English.

5. OTHER INFLUENCES ON ENGLISH

Undoubtedly there has been of late a great quickening of interest in English as a *spoken* language, to which the art of broadcasting has made substantial contributions. It is too soon to say whether the cinema will leave any permanent marks on the language. Since its appeal is so largely visual, it can hardly be of anything like the significance of the radio which deals only by the spoken word. Moreover, so far, its influence seems to be only in slang and cant terms and expressions which have scarcely reached as far as good colloquial usage. Perhaps an exception to this generalization is the new meaning of the word *picture*. A recent social survey inquirer found in one area that people who were asked what pictures they liked best, took it for granted that the question referred to films. 'To go to the pictures' is as frequently heard as 'to go to the cinema'.

One effect of universal schooling is the weakening of regional dialect and the growth of 'modified' standard English in imitation of teachers and through their efforts after producing the 'received standard'. Many children now shew a sort of 'bilingualism', speaking one form of English at home and another at school. Some teachers, instead of concentrating on training clarity and grace of speech and sensitive linguistic observation together with understanding of and admiration for the best models, tend to expend energy on eradicating dialectal sounds and intonation, giving children the impression that a local dialect is necessarily 'inferior' or 'uncultured'. This may result in unnatural types of speech, linguistic snobbishness and a seeking after artificial refinement which has no foundation in the personality of the speaker. 'Good English' must be talked naturally, or it is not good. The necessity of acquiring a form of 'received' English for the sake of convenience when mixing in society or working in different areas, is something quite distinct from any question of the 'superiority' of one dialect over another. Southern English based on that of educated London has become the accepted model in England for historical reasons; and hence its choice by the B.B.C. for broadcasting in England or to users of English in the outer world. But other dialects have their excellences, such as vividness of phrase or apt words: nor is there any sure criterion for preferring one sound to another on grounds of pleasurableness.

Another tendency in the attitude to English which is having some effect, is what might perhaps be called the revival of grammar. After the war of 1914 to 1918, there was a marked movement in the schools against the teaching of formal grammar, as indeed against any sort of linguistic self-discipline. With the decay of direct understanding of the ancient classical languages and the knowledge that English could not fully and exactly be explained or described in the terms and within the rules traditionally set out for Latin, there came a desire to cast aside the restraints of grammatical teaching altogether.

We have seen earlier how it came about that the

serious academic study of the English vernacular
came into the hands of Latinate schoolmasters who
established the tradition of formal grammar which
has largely remained in England. But, while many
things in English are unsuited to be described in the
terminology originally invented for Latin grammar,
and the leaning to a Latin standard in syntax has
often been a check to natural usage, as we have seen,
it is also true that no better terminology has yet been
evolved. But the most serious result of this throwing
aside of the teaching of grammar was a general slack-
ness in the use of English, a loosening of style,
inaccurate or vague use of words, clichés, lack of
clarity in structure, etc. Moreover, there had been
good and natural grammar-books produced which set
forth the facts of the language while preserving such
of the traditional terms as were still convenient. On
coming to realize the growing ill-effects of this loss of
linguistic discipline, most authorities have lately been
insisting once more on some teaching of English
grammar. Grammar is only the attempt exactly to
describe the facts of a given language, and formulates
rules and definitions to clarify the understanding and
application by users of the language of these facts.
Without this knowledge which has been laboriously
put together by others with more leisure, the dis-
ciplined use of the language to its full capacity
becomes impossible to most people. Linguistic self-
control and aim, such as the teaching of formal
English grammar can give, is, in fact, generally
necessary for the development of powers of effective
self-expression, as the results of the absence of this
teaching between the two world wars has shewn.
Nor has the creation of an entirely new grammatical

terminology met with much success. For this merely replaces the traditional terms, which were, like all human efforts, inaccurate, by new descriptions which lack the convenience of tradition without avoiding new inaccuracies.

6. ENGLISH AS A WORLD LANGUAGE

The vast expansion of English cultural and commercial influence in many parts of the world, together with the more recent dominance of the material civilization of the United States of America, has suggested to many that English might well become the international auxiliary language of the world. An international language, as commonly conceived, is not in any sense a substitute for existing tongues, but simply to be used as a secondary language for the rapidly growing needs of understanding and intercourse between persons of different nationality. This is not the place to discuss the desirability of such an international language, at which many attempts have already been made. The drawback to these artificial or invented forms of speech and writing, even the best of them such as Esperanto, is that they are deliberate scientific constructions, yet intended to serve the purpose in some degree of what is fundamentally a natural and ever-changing growth. 'Languages' like Esperanto or Novial (another more recent example) are not living organisms as a real language is: for they are selectively made up out of existing speech-elements from the most familiar tongues, and tend to become quickly static. For such reasons it has been thought by others that it would be better to choose an already existing tongue for the world-language: and hence the question of English arises because of its already vast influence.

Two kinds of difficulty have been encountered by the advocates of English as a world language:—first its vast and complex vocabulary, and second, the lack of relationship between its spelling and its pronunciation. Two fairly notable schemes have been evolved for dealing with these: *Basic English* and *Anglic.*

Basic English, invented by Mr. C. K. Ogden and experimented with successfully (it is claimed) in several parts of the world, especially China, has received much attention in England, and during the latter years of the world war of 1939–45 was even made an official scheme by the British Government, which adopted the proposal without consulting English philologists. It consists of the 850 words thought necessary for expressing the minimum of things and thoughts required for simple international intercourse, and claims to be able to give what is needed for translating any prose (the Bible for example) into English that is intelligible to all peoples. To these 850 words are added common international technical terms like *hotel* or *radio*; and when any particular subject having its own technical terms such as a science is concerned, a special list of technical terms is added. Verbs, except a minimum of 'motor words' like *take* and *give*, are eliminated, their functions being performed by these 'motor words' plus the appropriate noun. The resulting 'language' is easy to learn, but lacks the qualities of a language in the usually accepted sense of the term: for like Esperanto or Novial, Basic English is a scientific selection and no natural growth, nor does it seem to have the living quality of the English from which it has been extracted. Its syntax is artificial perforce, and not that of English. Of late this Basic English, the rights in whose original work have been purchased by the British Government without any undertaking to make use of them, has seemed less to interest the public than in its earlier years. Its main intention was to avoid the great difficulty of the vast English vocabulary.

The extraordinary difficulties of English spelling for foreigners are supposed to be met by *Anglic*, invented in Sweden and perfected by an outstanding philologist, the late Professor R. E. Zachrisson. It avoids the unnaturalness of Basic English, while concentrating its efforts on simplifying English spelling on phonetic lines without making too many revolutionary departures from tradition. Spelling-reform, in view of the fixing of English orthography by the printers while the pronunciation has very greatly changed, has been worked at by many since the late sixteenth century; so that the aims of Anglic are not new, but perhaps pursued more scientifically than the same ends by other reformers. But, as has been said earlier, English must continue to change: and there are advantages in having a partly symbolic or ideographic spelling which does not depend entirely on sound. A 'phonetic spelling' becomes out of date with the changing pronunciation of the language: and a fixed traditional orthography having been so well established, it may be doubted whether the effort is worth making. Moreover, a spelling in accord with pronunciation would have to vary in the different parts of the world with the varying pronunciation of heterogeneous speakers. The experience, too, of some countries where the spelling has been reformed by Act of Parliament, does not always encourage such attempts. Norway, for instance, has changed her spelling officially thrice within living memory, and so far the result has been somewhat confusing, since the human users of the new orthographies have not been so scientific as the rapidly changing reformers. Whatever the cause, it does not appear that Anglic has been able to get itself at all effectively accepted in the world generally so far.

Language is a social activity: and whether it is really desirable for English or any other language—real or invented—to become a world-medium, is a question which perhaps concerns the anthropologist and other students of the 'social sciences' rather than the student of the English language.

CHAPTER VIII

AIMS AND METHODS OF STUDY

I. GENERAL CONSIDERATIONS

IT is hoped that the foregoing chapters will have indicated and stimulated something of the interest of the study of the English language, as well as shewn its very great importance. Let us now try to state what should be some of the aims and results of the study, and some methods by which it may be pursued further. To this end it will also be found profitable to notice how the subject has been treated in the past, and some outstanding scholars whose work has especially forwarded it. In order to set the student well on the way to a wider and deeper study of the English language, the whole will be concluded with suggestions for further reading.

First among the aims of the discipline outlined in this book may be placed the greatly enhanced appreciation and understanding of the masterpieces of English literature of different periods. Only in such a way can we see the literature of the country clear and whole. The aesthetic appreciation of Shakespeare or Milton is immensely quickened by an understanding of their language. Their rhymes become significant in assessing their craftsmanship through the study of their pronunciation; the exact shades of meaning of their words and phrases become clear only through the consciousness of the semantic changes in the language; only by a knowledge of the general character and idiom of the English of their respective times can we decide how far each was individual in this or that matter.

Secondly, the 'diachronic' or historical study of the language, enabling us as it does to see English as a whole—from the days of Cædmon, the first known English poet in the late seventh century, to the popular newspaper article of to-day, presents us with a picture of English civilization in its entirety. 'Each word has its history', said one of the greatest of French philologists; and in the words of a language one may trace the whole of the social development of its speakers down the ages. The originally Dutch military phrase from which our *forlorn hope* has developed with changed sense, reminds us of the Spanish wars of the Netherlands in the sixteenth century in which so many English volunteers took part; and the word *boycott* recalls the struggles over the Irish land question of the last century, in which Captain Boycott, isolated from all help by his enraged tenants, brought into being this now ordinary word.

Thirdly, we should strive to make both a 'diachronic' and a 'synchronic' study of the language. The diachronic study of the language of any period, including the English of to-day, brings out so many features which a static study of only the contemporary usage would have left undetected. Just as it is only possible fully to understand what Shakespeare did for the drama in the light of the work of those who went before him, so too his language cannot be fully grasped save with a knowledge of that of his forerunners. Much of the most respectable literary criticism has been spoilt by the neglect of the critics to study the language diachronically. They have written of the sounds of Milton's poetry or of the Authorized

Version of the Bible as if these works had been composed to be pronounced with the noises of the English of the twentieth century, or have assumed that Chaucer's words which have remained in the language were used by him in the sense they bear to-day. In short, the danger to just appreciation arises especially from unconsciously taking a static view of language. Equally, however, one should study each period just as its language stands, without the preconceived ideas and subjective expectations that come from a knowledge of history. There are aspects of the English of to-day which will be missed or misunderstood if they are not examined synchronically, that is quite apart from any knowledge of what may have caused them or led up to them. The word *wind* had a long vowel till late in the eighteenth century, and up to the middle of the nineteenth (because poetry always tends to be slower in change than prose) it could only rhyme with words like *mind* and *find*: but to pronounce it as [waind] in a piece of poetry of to-day because of the archaic dignity suggested by knowledge of the past, would be to misrepresent the facts. We must study both diachronically and synchronically, and yet examine the given portion of language separately from either point of view before coming to a final conclusion.

Fourthly, the discipline of studying one's own language throughout, sharpens the faculty of linguistic observation and increases one's appreciation of the importance of accuracy in the employment of words. This will strengthen and clarify one's powers in using English for all kinds of purposes. Looseness and vain repetition are common weaknesses among speakers and writers of to-day; and never has it been so needful to try to overcome and control that 'copious vagueness' in the English vocabulary to which Dr. Johnson drew attention. The dictionary, to which most people turn for final guidance, is no substitute for a first-hand knowledge and assimilation of all the great qualities of English.

Finally, the study of the language, with its so many varied aspects, is in itself a stimulus intellectually and also a pleasure. It enables one to explore its past riches for oneself, and opens the way to a large number of subsidiary studies. Of these latter may be mentioned place-names and dialects. Many an interesting word which once existed but has escaped written record, survives as an element in some place-name: but the digging out of these and the discovery of the history and derivation of the name, only become possible to the student who can look into the earlier documents in which old forms, which give the key to meaning and origin, lie hidden. Similarly, much of intrinsic value and real interest lies concealed in the dialects of Britain. Words that have vividness and colour, expressions that help us to understand obscure things in the development of the standard language, etc., will reward the student of dialect. The *Philological Society*, which has been at work for over a hundred years and under whose direction the great *New English Dictionary* was carried through, is now in process of making a survey of the dialects of Britain; and this is a field in which the humblest student of the English language may make his contribution.

2. METHODS OF STUDY

The first thing to be done by the student of the English language is to get a clear idea of the main principles of language-study. This may be done by reading such works as those of Sweet, Sapir, Vendryes and Bloomfield listed at the end of this chapter. Then these principles should be related to ways of thinking and philosophy, as is well illustrated in Urban's book *Language and Reality*, and in the general introductory portions of Sweet's *A New English Grammar.*

The next step should be a clear understanding of the main points in general phonetics and a mastering of the alphabet of the *International Phonetic Association* (that in general use). Thus the student will avoid the dangers of confusing spelling with pronunciation, or the written symbol with the sound. He will also be able, with a little practice, to write down any sound he hears accurately, and to translate the phonetic representations he sees of various pronunciations in books into the appropriate noises. This can be done by working over such a small book as Daniel Jones's *The Pronunciation of English*, which also provides practising exercises with key.

Then a formal historical grammar such as that of Sweet should be attempted, followed by a straightforward history of the language such as those of Baugh in America or the late H. C. Wyld in England.

Before undertaking the necessary reading of different types of English of the several periods to illustrate and drive home what has been learned from histories of English, the student should now try to cultivate the habit of using *The Shorter Oxford English Dictionary*. This is on historical lines, and shews the differing senses words have had during the whole Modern English period. After some practice in using this as a companion to his reading, the student should learn to work for the more difficult or interesting words in *The New English Dictionary*, whose ten large volumes cover the whole development of the language since the twelfth century, and include the etymologies or Old English originals for all. Since this great dictionary took over half a century to build and was completed in 1928, for the many new words and meanings which have come into the language in more recent years, one must consult its *Supplementary* volume published in 1933. The fascinating study of etymology can be explored in Skeat's *Principles of English Etymology*.

It will now be profitable for the student whose studies have reached thus far to try to read at least a small quantity of texts from all periods of the language in their original form. For without having some first-hand acquaintance with characteristic original texts, any information that can be acquired by reading books about the history of the language will remain a mere collection of 'right opinions' and will never become 'knowledge'. Only by seeing language in action, so to speak, can a feeling for it be attained, as distinct from a mere handling of the words which are its components. The student is advised, therefore, to work through, such a book first as Henry Sweet's *Anglo-Saxon Primer*, and his *First Steps in Anglo-Saxon*. This may be followed up by the easier pieces in Sweet's *Anglo-Saxon Reader* or Wyatt's *Anglo-Saxon Reader*. For Middle English, Sweet's *First* and *Second Primers of Middle English* may be followed by A. S. Cook's *Literary Middle English Reader*. Thus some knowledge will have been gained, not only of the main types of the language before the age of printing, but also of outstanding specimens of mediaeval English literature. For the Modern period, a selection should be made from literary masterpieces, taking care to read them as far as possible in their original spelling and wording (for so many of the commoner editions have been modernized).

The books mentioned in the last paragraph all have glossaries and technical introductions, which make them up to a point self-contained. But, as remarked above, *The New English Dictionary* should be used for special difficulties, and *The Shorter Oxford Dictionary* kept beside one as a constant companion.

Having now arrived at a grasp of general linguistic principles, the uses of the phonetic method of transcription, some ability to use a dictionary made on historical lines, and having read for oneself at least some typical specimens of the English language chosen from each of its main periods, one may now take up again some general histories of the language profitably and with confidence. Such general yet scholarly works as those of H. C. Wyld (particularly his *Historical Study of the Mother Tongue*), A. Baugh, Henry Bradley, O. Jespersen and Emerson are suggested, though none of these is complete or final in any sense. Then, for more serious study may come Sweet's great *New English Grammar*, which provides the foundation of grammatical principles, a historical survey of the language, and an introduction to modern syntax. Dr. C. T. Onions' little book on English syntax should follow, since it remains the authoritative masterpiece in its kind.

The student who gets as far as completing the foregoing course of study, will be in a position to decide for himself how best to proceed further: for he will have discovered where in the subject his particular interests lie, and will know how to pursue them with the necessary preliminary equipment. From *The Cambridge Bibliography of English Literature*'s section on the English language, he will be able to see exactly what has been published both in general on the subject, and on all its branches.

3. SOME ENGLISH LANGUAGE STUDIES OF THE PAST

From the early sixteenth century, with the revitalized interest in the vernacular aroused by Renaissance influences, men began to write books on the improvement of English spelling, on pronunciation and on English rhetoric. The first dictionaries for foreign languages began to appear at this time; and with the next century the first grammars proper. Ben Jonson wrote an English grammar, and more professional teachers, like Alexander Gill (Milton's schoolmaster), with his *Logonomia Anglica* (1621), Charles Butler (1634), and C. Cooper (1685). All of these except Butler's *English Grammar* were written in Latin. The whole of the early Modern period abounds with works (some of them ephemeral) on matters of pronunciation and spelling-improvements. Palsgrave (1530) did much for English as well as for French linguistic knowledge with his explanation of French, his *Lesclarcissement de la langue françoyse*; and a number of schoolmasters such as J. Bellot and George Mason wrote French works on English grammar which throw much light on the English of the time. The eighteenth century was a great period (in quantity) in grammar-books, and Dr. Johnson supplied his *Dictionary* both with an English grammar and an outline of the history of the language. The interest in provincial dialect is shewn as early as 1679 by a *glossary of North-Country words* which still has value, by Ray. The story of the development of English dictionaries has been told in Chapter II.

The dissolution of the monasteries, which revealed to the few keen searchers a number of Old and Middle English MSS. from the monastic libraries, coupled with the new theological zeal engendered by the Reformation, caused the first studies in Anglo-Saxon to be made. The first Anglo-Saxon printed book appeared as a kind of Protestant tract in 1567 as *The Testimony of Antiquity concerning the Church in England*, a rendering, with the original text and a polemical preface of Ælfric's homily on the Easter Eucharist. But some of the new theologians, both Protestant and Catholic, were scholars who became interested in the language and literature of Old England for their own sake. Archbishop Parker and his still more learned secretary Joscelyn did much for Old English scholarship in collecting MSS. and causing books to be published and edited; and Laurence Nowell, Dean of Lichfield, was the first known possessor of the MS. of *Beowulf* and himself left collections for an Old English dictionary. The seventeenth century was one of great progress and learning, in which Old English began to be taught both at Cambridge and Oxford. By its close, Edward Thwaites, Fellow of Queen's College, Oxford, could boast that he had fifteen students 'proficient in the Saxon tongue'. In 1706 George Hickes published his great *Treasury of Ancient Northern Languages* (still in Latin) with grammars and many texts of Old English and Old Norse; and this was accompanied by a most scholarly catalogue by Humphrey Wanley of the extant Old English MSS. The same Hickes had provided as early as 1689 the first Old English grammar, which remained the model for more than a century. The next century saw further developments and a great extension of interest, particularly towards its end, in earlier English.

But it was in the early nineteenth century that great Anglo-Saxon scholars became fairly frequent, such as Benjamin Thorpe, John Kemble and those whom they inspired. These two provided collections of charters, edited texts and made advances in grammar and archaeology.

Till now all Old English texts had been printed in the original character based on Irish Latin. But soon after the middle of the century the practice of printing in Roman letters which still persists, became general. General Indo-European philology had been put on the scientific road by Sir William Jones, the judge and scholar in India, in the late eighteenth century, and the work had been systematized in Germany by the great Jakob Grimm (also part-author of the famous *Fairytales*) in the first half of the nineteenth. But it was Henry Sweet (1845–1912) who laid the foundations of the study of Old English dialects, scientific Old English lexicography (good work had been done as far back as the seventeenth century by Junius and Sumner), of English historical grammar, and of applied phonetics. He was also the greatest English general linguist and philologist, and the best writer of elementary Old English and Middle English books for beginners. The last half of the nineteenth century was something like a golden age for English linguistic studies. *The*

Philological Society, founded in 1841, set to work on its great dictionary, and had as its active members, besides Sweet, Sir James Murray, who founded its *New English Dictionary*, and F. J. Furnivall, who founded *The Early English Text Society*, *The Chaucer Society* and several others of the kind, and was the inspiration of almost every kind of English mediaeval and philological effort. Henry Bradley, also of the Philological Society and the New English Dictionary, was a pioneer in the study of place-names which is now carried on with regular publications by *The Place-name Society*. From among holders of the professorship of Anglo-Saxon at Oxford (founded in the eighteenth century) at this time, Joseph Bosworth who made the Old English dictionary on which the later revised largest work of the kind is based, and John Earle, who wrote the first small and readable book on philology in English and edited texts of several kinds, may here be mentioned: and from those of the parallel chair at Cambridge, Walter Skeat stands out as the most prolific editor of Old English and Middle English texts and the founder of modern Chaucerian editing (to which Thomas Tyrwhitt had well contributed in the previous century).

Perhaps the first outstanding scholarly and satisfying work on the history of the English language was Sweet's *History of English Sounds* (1881), and the first complete and also philosophical and historical English grammar was also his *A New English Grammar*. But by the close of the nineteenth century English philology was beginning to be taught in the universities, and names and works of outstanding value become too numerous for listing here. Probably the greatest contributions of the nineteenth century to philology from the more general point of view were the founding of the knowledge of applied phonetics by Sweet, of the history of pronunciation by A. J. Ellis, and of the scientific study of dialects in England by Joseph Wright, who a little later published his *Dialect Dictionary*.

No complete history of the English language has yet been written. The task is too vast and heterogeneous for one man to attempt; and it would perhaps be impossible to find a group of scholars of enough community of spirit and outlook to carry through such a work. It is also true that while modern universities almost all teach the subject (and hence provide a public for technical works), the conditions of modern life make the number of devoted scholars with the necessary leisure and means for the study and for the carrying out of large projects, tend very much to decrease. On the other hand, if the energy and enthusiasm of so many educated laymen who now are beginning to interest themselves in the English language or some of its by-paths, could be directed and encouraged by a little more discipline and concentration, it may be hoped that the material for the complete history of the language may yet be provided—if not put together. There is, outside the academic world of often over-driven students, a large educated public possessed of some leisure: and if some of these people can be persuaded by this little book to give themselves the pleasure and the discipline of a further course of study along the lines suggested in the previous section of this chapter, the writer will feel that he has spent his own scanty leisure well in making it.

4. SELECT BIBLIOGRAPHY

What follows is a short list of books proposed for carrying on the study to those who have been interested enough in this book. It is in no sense anything more than a small selection of books that seem to be among the most helpful. It is arranged below under the respective chapters of the book.

CHAPTER I

(a) GENERAL WORKS ON LANGUAGE AND LINGUISTICS. (Alphabetical)

Bloomfield, L.: *Language*. (London, 1935.)

Jespersen, O.: *Language, its Nature, Development and Origin*. (London, 1923.)

Jespersen, O.: *Progress in Language*. (London, 1894.)

Meillet, A.: *Linguistique Historique et Linguistique Générale*. (Paris, 1921.)

Ogden, C. K., and Richards, I. A.: *The Meaning of Meaning*. (London, 1923.)

Sapir, E.: *Language*. (New York, 1921.)

Sweet, H.: *The History of Language*. (London, 1900.)

Urban, L.: *Language and Reality*. (New York, 1935.)

(b) OUTLINE WORKS ON THE ENGLISH LANGUAGE. (In order of date)

Emerson, O. F.: *The History of the English Language*. (New York, 1894.)

Bradley, H.: *The Making of English*. (London, 1904.)

Jespersen, O.: *Growth and Structure of the English Language*. (Leipzig, 1919.)

Classen, E.: *Outlines of the History of the English Language*. (Manchester, 1919.)

McKnight, G. and R.: *Modern English in the Making*. (New York, 1928.)

Baugh, A.: *History of the English Language*. (New York, 1935.)

Mossé, F.: *Esquisse d'une Histoire de la Langue anglaise.* (Lyons, 1947.)

Onions, C. T.: 'The English Language' in *The Character of England*, ed. Barker. (Oxford, 1947.)

CHAPTER II

(*a*) GENERAL WORKS ON VOCABULARY. (Alphabetical)

Barfield, O.: *History in English Words.* (London, 1926.)

Groom, B.: *A Short History of English Words.* (London, 1926.)

Greenough and Kittredge: *Words and their Ways in English Speech.* (New York, 1900.)

McKnight, G.: *English Words and their Background.* (New York, 1923.)

Serjeantson, Mary: *A History of the Foreign Words in English.* (London, 1935.)

Skeat, W.: *Principles of English Etymology.* (Oxford, 1887 and 1892.)

(*b*) DICTIONARIES AND GLOSSARIES. (In order of importance)

A New English Dictionary on Historical Principles, ed. by Sir James Murray, Henry Bradley, Sir William Craigie and C. T. Onions. (Oxford, 1884–1928.)

Supplement to the above, ed. W. A. Craigie and C. T. Onions. (Oxford, 1933.)

The Shorter Oxford English Dictionary, ed. C. T. Onions. (Oxford, 1932.)

Skeat, W.: *An Etymological Dictionary of the English Language.* (Oxford, 1898.)

Wyld, H. C.: *The Universal Dictionary of the English Language.* (London, 1932.)

CHAPTER III

WORKS ON SPELLING AND PRONUNCIATION. (Alphabetical)

Bradley, H.: On the Relation between Spoken and written English, in his *Collected Papers*, ed. Bridges. (Oxford, 1923.)

Ellis, A. J.: *On Early English Pronunciation.* (London 1869–89.)

Jones, Daniel: *English Pronunciation.* (London, 1919.)

Jones, Daniel: *An English Pronouncing Dictionary.* (London, 1923.)

Karlgren, B.: *Sound and Symbol in Chinese.* (London, 1923.)

Sweet, H.: *The Practical Study of Language.* (New York, 1900.)

Sweet, H.: *The Sounds of English.* (Oxford, 1910.)

Ward, I., and Armstrong, L.: *Handbook of English Intonation.* (Cambridge, 1926.)

Wrenn, C. L.: 'The Value of Spelling as Evidence.' (*Transactions of the Philological Society*, London, 1944.)

Wyld, H. C.: *A History of Modern Colloquial English*, 3rd ed., revised (Oxford, Blackwell, 1936.)

Viëtor, W.: *Shakespeare's Pronunciation.* (Marburg, 1906.)

Zachrisson, R.: *Pronunciation of English Vowels, 1400 to 1700.* (Gothenburg, 1913.)

CHAPTER IV

(a) HISTORICAL GRAMMARS. (Alphabetical)

Jespersen, O.: *A Modern English Grammar on Historical Principles.* (Heidelberg, 1909, unfinished.)

Morris, R.: *Historical Outlines of English Accidence*, revised by Kellner and Bradley. (London, 1895.)

Sweet, H.: *A New English Grammar, Logical and Historical*, Part I. (Oxford, 1892.)

Sweet, H.: *A History of English Sounds*, 2nd ed. (Oxford, 1888.)

Wright, J and E.: *An Elementary Old English Grammar.* (Oxford.)

Wright, J. and E.: *An Elementary Middle English Grammar.* (Oxford.)

Wright, J. and E.: *An Elementary New English Grammar.* (Oxford.)

(b) BOOKS CONTAINING TEXTS WITH APPARATUS FOR
        BEGINNERS. (Alphabetical)

> Cook, A. S.: *A Literary Middle English Reader*.
>   (London, 1921.)
> Sisam, K.: *Fourteenth Century Verse and Prose*.
>   (Oxford.)
> Sweet, H.: *An Anglo-Saxon Primer*. (Oxford.)
> Sweet, H.: *First Steps in Anglo-Saxon*. (Oxford.)
> Sweet, H.: *An Anglo-Saxon Reader*, 11th ed., revised
>   by C. T. Onions. (Oxford, 1948.)
> Sweet, H.: *A First Middle English Primer*. (Oxford.)
> Sweet, H.: *A Second Middle English Primer*. (Oxford.)

(c) DIALECTS. (Alphabetical)

> Ellis, A. J.: *Early English Pronunciation*, last vol.
>   (London, 1889.)
> Skeat, W.: *English Dialects*. (Cambridge, 1911.)
> Wright, J.: *The English Dialect Dictionary*. (Oxford,
>   1898–1905.)
> Wright, J.: *An English Dialect Grammar*. (Oxford.)

CHAPTER V

WORKS ON ENGLISH SYNTAX. (Alphabetical)

> Curme, G.: 'Syntax', Vol. 3 of his and Kurath's *A
>   Grammar of the English Language*. (New York,
>   1931.)
> Kellner, L.: *Historical Outlines of English Syntax*.
>   (London, 1892.)
> Kruisinga, E. A.: *Handbook of Present-day English*.
>   (5 vols., Groningen, 1914–26.)
> Onions, C. T.: *Advanced English Syntax*. (London,
>   5th ed., 1929.)
> Poutsma, H. A.: *Grammar of Late Modern English*,
>   Part 2. (3 vols., Groningen, 1931–2.)
> Sweet, H.: 'Syntax', Part II of his *New English
>   Grammar*. (Oxford, 1899.)

CHAPTER VI

(a) SHAKESPEARE

> Onions, C. T.: *A Shakespeare Glossary*. (Oxford.)

Schmidt, A.: *A Shakespeare-Lexicon*. (Berlin, 1902.)

Abbott, E.: *Shakespearean Grammar*. (London, revised 1870.)

Onions, C. T.: 'Shakespeare's Language', in *Nine Plays of Shakespeare*, ed. George Gordon. (Oxford.)

Gordon, G.: 'Shakespeare's English', *Society for Pure English Tract* No. 29. (Oxford.)

Willcock, Gladys: *Shakespeare as a Critic of Language*, Shakespeare Association pamphlet. (London, 1936.)

Willcock, Gladys: 'Shakespeare and Rhetoric', in *Essays and Studies by Members of the English Association* for 1945. (Oxford.)

(*b*) THE BIBLE

The Bible in its Ancient and Modern Versions, ed. Wheeler Robinson. (London, 1944.)

Tyndale's New Testament, ed. H. Wallis. (Cambridge, 1936.)

(*c*) SOME OUTSTANDING POETS. (Chronological order)

Wrenn, C. L.: On Re-reading the Shepheardes Calender (of Spenser), in *Essays and Studies by Members of the English Association* for 1944. (Oxford.)

Darbishire, Helen: *The MS. of Milton's Paradise Lost Book I*, with transcription and introduction on the spelling. (Oxford.)

Tillyard, M.: *The Miltonic Setting*. (Cambridge, 1939.)

Tillotson, G.: *Pope*, the chapter on his diction. (London, 1938.)

Wordsworth: *Prefaces and Essays* included in the Oxford edition of his poetical Works. (Oxford.)

CHAPTER VII

RECENT BOOKS ON VARIOUS TOPICS. (Alphabetical)

Herbert, A. P.: *What a Word*. (London, 1935.)

Horwill, J.: *A Dictionary of American Usage*. (Oxford, 1935.)

Krapp, G.: *The English Language in America*. (New York, 1923.)

Mencken, J.: *The American Language*. (New York, revised 1938.)

Lloyd James, A.: *The Broadcast Word.* (London, 1935.)

Straumann, H.: *Newspaper Headlines*. (London, 1935.)

CHAPTER VIII

(*a*) FURTHER WORKS ON THE ENGLISH LANGUAGE

Huchon, R.: *Histoire de la Langue Anglaise*, Vols. 1 and 2. (Paris, 1923 and 1930.)

Sweet, H.: *A Short Historical English Grammar.* (Oxford.)

Wyld, H. C.: *The Historical Study of the Mother Tongue.* (London, 1913.)

(*b*) FURTHER WORKS ON LANGUAGE THEORY AND HISTORY

Bréal, M.: *Essai de Semantique*. (4th ed., Paris, 1908.)

De Saussure, F.: *Cours de Linguistique générale.* (Paris, 1923.)

Gardiner, Sir Alan: *Speech and Language*. (2nd ed., Oxford, 1951.)

Palmer, L. R.: *An Introduction to Modern Linguistics.* (Macmillan, 1936.)

Hjelmslev, L.: *Principes de Grammaire générale.* (Copenhagen, 1928.)

Jespersen, O.: *The Philosophy of Grammar.* (London, 1924.)

Stern, O.: *Meaning and Change of Meaning.* (Gothenburg, 1932.)

Pedersen, H.: *Linguistic Science in the 19th Century*, translated by J. Spargo. (Cambridge, Mass., U.S.A., 1931.)

(*c*) FURTHER OLD AND MIDDLE ENGLISH READERS

Morris and Skeat: *Specimens of Early English*, Parts 1, 2 and 3. (Oxford.)

Dickins and R. Wilson.: *Early Middle English Reader.* (Bowes & Bowes, Cambridge, 1951.)

Hall, J.: *Selections from Early Middle English.* (Oxford.)

Wyatt, A. J.: *Anglo-Saxon Reader.* (Cambridge.)

Sedgfield, W.: *An Anglo-Saxon Verse Book.* (Manchester, 1922.)

(d) SPECIAL SMALLER PERIOD DICTIONARIES

Clark Hall, J.: *A Concise Anglo-Saxon Dictionary.* (Cambridge.)

Sweet, H.: *A Student's Dictionary of Anglo-Saxon.* (Oxford.)

Mayhew and Skeat: *A Concise Middle English Dictionary.* (Oxford.)

Stratmann and Bradley: *A Middle English Dictionary.* (Oxford.)

(e) PLACE-NAME STUDIES

Mawer, A.: *Problems in Place-name Study.* (Cambridge, 1929.)

Ekwall, E.: *The Oxford Dictionary of English Place-names.* (Oxford.)

The English Place-name Society: Introduction to the *Survey of English Place-names.* (Cambridge, 1924.)

(f) BIBLIOGRAPHIES FOR FULLER REFERENCE

The Cambridge Bibliography of English Literature, section on the English Language, Vol. I, pp. 24–49. (Cambridge, 1940.)

Kennedy, A. G.: *A Bibliography of Writings on the English Language.* (New Haven, U.S.A., 1927.)

(g) SOME EARLY ENGLISH GRAMMARIANS

Palsgrave, J.: *Lesclarcissement de la langue françoyse,* 1530, ed. Genin. (Paris, 1852.)

Hart, J.: 'An Orthographie', in Jespersen's *John Hart's Pronunciation of English.* (Heidelberg,1907.)

Bellot, J.: *Le Maistre d'escole anglois,* 1580, ed. Spira. (Halle, 1912.)

Gill, A.: *Logonomia Anglica,* 1621, ed. Jiriczek. (Halle, 1903.)

Butler, C.: *English Grammar,* 1634, ed. Eichler. (Halle, 1910.)

Walker, J.: *Rhetorical Grammar.* (London, 1801.)

Hickes, G.: *Institutiones Grammaticae Anglo-Saxonicae et Moeso-Gothicae.* (Oxford, 1689.)

SUBJECT INDEX

accents, 144
accidence, 107, 130
adjectives, 136
Ælfric, 40–42, 91, 113
Albanian, 12
Angles, 20, 22, 37
Anglic, 204
Anglo-Saxon, 20–24
approach, diachronic, 134, **135**
   synchronic, 134, 135
Arabic, 78
archaism, 127–129
Armenian, 12
Aryan, 10, 11
Auden, 180

Bailey, Nathan, 99
Balto-Slavic, 12
Barnes, William, 42, 83, 178
Bible, Authorized Version,
   150–153, 165
   Calvinists' Geneva, 152
   Douai-Rheims, 152
Bridges, Robert, 171, 179
British Broadcasting Corpora-
   tion, 97, 195
Browne, Sir Thomas, 47
Burke, 182–184
Byrhtferth, 40

cases, 135, 136, 140–142
Cawdrey, Robert, 98
Caxton, 27, 94, 95, 121
Celtic, 12, 75
Centum-Languages, 12
Chaucer, 56, 91, 105, 112, 123,
   124, 128, 129, 148, 165,
   166
Churchill, W. S., 182–184
Cockney, 26

Common European, 50, 67, 68,
   74, 76
Common Germanic, 15
Cooper, Thomas, 98
Czech, 77

Dekker, 71
dialects, East Midland, 121
   Northern, 120–122
   regional, 189
   Southern, 121
   West Midland, 121
dictionaries, 98–101
Donne, 180
Dryden, 59, 61, 96, 140, **141,**
   148, 150, 167–168
Dutch, 68–72
   South African, 72

East Midland, 27
English, American, 190–194
   Basic, 83, 203
   Early Modern, 28
   Good, 44, 188, 189, 200
   Later Modern, 28
   Middle, 22, 25, 26
   Modern, 22, 27
   modified standard, 189
   New, 23, 28
   Old, 20–24
   Present-day, 28
   received standard, 187–188
etymologies, 98

Finno-Ugrian, 14
Flemish, 69–72
forms, 130
French, 52–62
   Norman, 53–**55**
   Northern, 52

Gaelic, Irish, 75
  Scottish, 75
  Welsh, 75
gender, common, 111
  grammatical, 110
  natural, 110
German, High, 21, 68
  Low, 21, 70, 71
Germani, 20
Germanic, 13–19
  Common, 15
  Primitive, 15
glossaries, 98
grammar, 200, 201
  historical, 135
Greek, 12, 48–52
  Classical, 49, 51

homonyms, 126
homophones, 126
  conflict of, 127
Hopkins, Gerard Manley, 179,
  180
Hungarian, 77

Indo-European, 10–16, 18
Indo-Germanic, 10, 11
Indo-Iranian, 12
inflexion, 7, 106, 143–145
intonation, 8, 109
Italian, 72, 73

Johnson, Dr. Samuel, 61, 96,
  99, 123, 125, 148, 150, 168
Junius, Francis, 99
Jutes, 20, 22, 37

Keats, 128
kenemes, 132
Kersey, John, 99
King Alfred, 21

language, 1–3
  agglutinative, 14
  emotive, 2, 4
  incorporating, 14
  indicative, 3, 4

  inner, 2, 3
  origin of, 5
  outer, 2, 3
  symbolic, 4, 5
Latin, 12, 37–48
  Christian, 39, 40
Lydgate, 129

Malory, 153
Mercian, 24
Midland, 24
  East, 27
Milton, 46, 47, 103, 123, 125,
  138, 170–175
morphology, 106, 130
Morris, William, 31

Norse, 25, 62–68

Ogden, C. K., 203, 204
optative, 131

participle, present, 142
Pecock, Reginald, 36
periphrases, 8
Persian, 79
Phillips, Edward, 98
philology, 30
phonetic spelling, 88
  writing, 85–87
phonetics, 85
phonology, 23, 106
Pitt, 182
pleremes, 132
Pope, 175, 176
Portuguese, 74
Prayer-Book, Anglican, 151
pronouns, interrogative, 139,
  140
  personal, 137
  relative, 139

radio, 194–199
Renaissance, 28
rhymes, 101–104
  eye-, 102
  spelling, 102

rhymes—*contd.*
  traditional, 102
  traditional spelling, 102
  true, 102
  true plus, 103
  visual, 102, 103
Richardson, Charles, 100
Russian, 77

Saint Dunstan, 40
Sanskrit, 79
Satem-languages, 12
Saxons, 20, 22, 37
Scott, 128
semantics, 30, 108
semasiology, 30, 108
Shakespeare, 31, 44, 73, 91,
    114, 125, 147–150, 156–164
Skinner, Stephen, 99
Slavonic, 76
South-Eastern, 24
speech, 2
spelling, ideographic, 88
  phonetic, 88
  Old English, 93
Spenser, 73, 103, 115, 128, 129,
    148, 166, 167, 180
Steele, 140

stress, 119
  end-, 119
  even, 119
  initial, 119
subjunctive, 131, 133, 138, 139
Swift, 96, 148
syntax, 107, 130–132

enses, 8
Teutonic, 20
Thackeray, 128
tonemes, 143
Tyndale, 150–154

Uralian, 14

verbs, strong, 19
  weak, 19
vowel shift, 91

Webster, Noah, 101
Wessex, 24
West-Saxon, 24
word-order, 7
Wordsworth, 148, 156, 175–
    178
Wyclif, 150

WORD INDEX

OLD ENGLISH

biscop, 38
bītan, 142
bīting, 142
bītinga, 142
bletsian, 39
burg, 53

cæster, 38
cāsere, 37
ceaster, 38
cerm, 122
cēse, 37
cild, 111
cuman, 93
cwēn, 127
cwene, 127
cyrice, 39, 93

dǣl-nimend, 41
Dene, 65
dēor, 125
drȳ, 75
dwīnan, 159

Ēastron, 39
Ēastru, 39
eggian, 66
-ende, 142
Engle, 22

Englisc, 21
eow, 137
-eþ, 131

felaga, 66
forsetennys, 41

gē, 137
gigant, 38
Gōdspell, 41

hālig, 57
handbōc, 83
heom, 137
hit, 137
hūs, 93, 111
hūsbonda, 66
hūsel, 31
husting, 66
hwā, 140
hwylc, 140

-ing, 62

lagu, 66
Legaceaster, 38
lufu, 93, 94

mæsse, 39
miht, 94
munuc, 38
mylen, 37
mynster, 38

nama, 41

orc, 38

prēost, 38

riht, 94

strǣt, 37

þæt, 139
þrǣll, 66
þrynes, 41

ūtlaga, 66

wīc, 111
wīcing, 62, 63
wīf, 111
wrang, 66

MIDDLE ENGLISH

acorden, 53
Aprill (Ch.), 56

Baptist, 55
basin, 55
bataille, 53, 55
beste, 55
bitinge, 142

canceler, 55
canun, 55
capelein, 55
Cardinal, 55
carited, 53, 55
castel, 55
chapel, 55
corages (Ch.), 56, 124

correcte (Ch.), 166
cours (Ch.), 56
croppes (Ch.), 124
cuntesse, 53
curt, 53

desputen, 55
dorring-do (Ch.), 129

engendred (Ch.), 56
faerie, 129
flour (Ch.), 56
foreste, 53
foules (Ch.), 124
furneis, 55

gentil (Ch.), 124
Grace, 55

hem (Ch.), 137
hous, 94

image, 55
-inde, 142
-inga, 142
-inge, 142
inspired (Ch.), 56

justise, 53

lamp, 55

licour (Ch.), 56, 124
loue, 94
luue, 94

Marche (Ch.), 56
market, 53
martyr (Ch.), 56
Maudeleyne (Ch.), 105
melodye (Ch.), 56
merci, 56
miracle, 53, 55
monk, 94

Nature (Ch.), 56

pais, 53
palmers (Ch.), 56
parfit (Ch.), 124
Passiun, 55
perced (Ch.), 56
pilgrimages (Ch.), 56
Prior, 55

prisun, 53, 55
processiun, 53
prophete, 55

religiun, 55
rent, 53

seint, 55
service, 55
sone, 94
specially (Ch.), 56
straunge (Ch.), 56

tendre (Ch.), 56
tresor, 53
tur, 53, 55

veine (Ch.), 56
veray (Ch.), 124
vertu (Ch.), 56, 124

werre, 55

MODERN ENGLISH

a-, 51
-able, 115
abroad, 118
abysmal, 48
academy, 50
acrobat, 49, 50
adjective, 83
admiral, 78
affection (Sh.), 157
agnostic, 50
aim at, 190
aim to (Amer.), 190
-al, 48, 50
album, 48
alcohol, 78
alcove, 78
ale, 52
algebra, 78
alibi, 48
Allah, 78

alphabet, 50
amateur, 58
amatory, 35
amber, 78
amok, 80
amoral, 51
anarch (Milton), 175
-ance, 115
and, 131
anealing (Sh.), 31
ante, 115
ante-date, 115
anti, 50
anti-British, 51
apparatus, 48
appendicitis, 49
arcade, 73
arctic, 171
are (Spenser), 103
area, 78

arena, 48
arre (Spenser), 103
arsenal, 78
artic (Milton), 171
artichoke, 73
assassin, 78
at, 131
-ate, 48
atom, 49, 50
attaché, 61
auspicious (Sh.), 44, 160
ayah, 75
azure, 79

babble, 151
bacillus, 48
back, 147
bagatelle, 58
ballet, 59

bamboo, 80
bangle, 79
banshee, 75
bant, 118
Banting, 118
bard, 75
barrage, 60
basimecu (Sh.), 159
basis, 50
bathe, 67
bathos, 50
baton, 60
beer, 52
beggars description (Sh.), 148
belles-lettres, 60
beret, 60
better, 21
Bible, 50
bishop, 38
bizarre, 58
blarney, 75
blatant, 129, 167
blattant (Spenser), 129
blatter, 129
bleak, 67
bless, 39
blitz, 81
blood-boltered (Sh.), 158
blue (Amer.), 193
board, 57
Boer, 72
bog, 75
Bolshevik, 76
bona fide, 116
bonus, 48
boomerang, 80
booze, 70, 71
boss, 71
both, 67
bought, 19, 20
boycott, 81, 207
bragadochio (Spenser), 167
brandy-wine, 70

bric-à-brac, 60
brigantine, 58
broadcast, 118
broccoli, 73
brochure, 60
brogue, 75
browned-off, 132
browned-offness, 132
brunette, 60
buffalo, 75
bulwark, 70
bump, 147, 160
bungalow, 79
buoy, 70
bureau, 60, 117
bureaucracy, 117
bureaucratic, 117
burlesque, 59
bus, 83
busk, 121
buy, 19, 20
by-spots (Wordsworth), 178

cache, 59
cairn, 75
calibre, 78
calleth, 78
calls, 121
cambric, 70
camouflage, 61, 80
cannibal, 74
canoe, 80
canteen, 60
canto (Spenser), 73
canyon, 74
casino, 73
caste, 75
-caster, 38
castigate (Sh.), 44, 160
cattle, 55
caucus (Amer.), 192
caustic, 50
-cester, 38
chagrin, 59
chair, 58

champagne, 59
chancellor, 55
chaplain, 55
character, 49
chargé d'affaires, 61
charity, 55, 154
charm (Milton), 122, 123, 174
chassis, 60
chattel, 55
chauffeur, 60
check, 79
check-mate, 79
cheese, 37
chef, 58, 60
Chester, 38
-chester, 38
cheval, 60
chic, 60
chiffonier, 60
childed (Sh.), 161
chimpanzee, 80
chit, 79
chorus, 49, 50
church, 39, 154
churm, 122
cinema, 118
cipher, 78, 125
circus, 48
clan, 75
claymore, 75
clerk (Amer.), 191
cliché, 60
clientèle, 61
clinic, 50
collect, 43
colleen, 75
commandeer, 72
communiqué, 60
communism, 84
complex, 48
conclusion, 163
concurrently, 50
condition, 116
congregation, 154
connoisseur, 58
contre-temps, 59

coquette, 59
coracle, 75
correct, 59, 166
corps, 60
corsair, 59
cortège, 59
coterie, 60
cotton, 78
coup, 60
court, 58
coy, 70
crag, 75, 121
crêpe, 60
cretonne, 60
critic (Sh.), 44, 160
critique, 60
crooked, 66
cross, 67
cul-de-sac, 60
cupola, 73
cushy, 79
cut (Amer.), 192
cycle, 49

-d (Milton), 171
D.V., 116
dactyls, 46
dago, 74
damsel, 153
Danes, 65
daring-hardy (Sh.),
    161
débâcle, 61
debts, 151
debutante, 60
deck, 70
décor, 59
decoy, 70
deer, 125
defendant, 54
deficit, 48
de-house, 116
de-louse, 116
démarche, 59
democracy, 84, 117
depot, 60
de-requisition, 116

derring-do, 129,
    (Spenser), 167
desire, 35
desperado, 74
Dickon, 162
dictaphone, 49
dilemma, 50
dilettante, 73
dinghy, 79
dingle, 122, (Milton),
    175
diocese, 43
diphthong, 50
dis-, 115
disappointed (Sh.), 31
disgusting, 125
disown, 115
distingué, 60
distraint, 54
diurnal (Milton), 178
do, 144
dock, 70
dogma, 50
dope, 71
dossier, 61
dote, 71
double-entendre, 59
dragoon, 59
drama, 50
dreary, 115
dreriment (Spenser),
    115
drill, 70
drive, 19
driven, 19
drove, 19
Druid, 75
drum, 118
dumb (Amer.), 193
dungaree, 79
dwindle (Sh.), 122,
    159, 162
dwine, 122

-e, 131, 138,
Easter, 39
ecstasy, 50

-ed (Milton), 174
educate, 48
egg, 66
ego, 48
eisteddfod, 75
elastic, 48
elder, 154
elegy, 50
élite, 60
'em, 137
em-, 161
embattle (Sh.), 161
embay'd (Sh.), 161
émigré, 60
emmesh (Sh.), 161
empoison (Sh.), 161
-en, 131, 138,
    (Milton), 171
en-, 161
enact (Sh.), 161
enchafed (Sh.), 161
enchas'd (Sh.), 161
endeared (Sh.), 161
enfree (Sh.), 161
engaol (Sh.), 161
engild (Sh.), 161
engirt (Sh.), 161
enkindle (Sh.), 161
enlink (Sh.), 161
enmesh (Sh.), 161
ennui, 60
en passant, 59
enrooted (Sh.), 161
enseamed (Sh.), 161
ensky (Sh.), 161
entame (Sh.), 161
epic, 50
equivalent, 43
-es, 121
espionage, 60
esplanade, 74
-eth, 121
etiquette, 60
evacuee, 81
executive (Amer.),
    193
executrix, 116

exit, 48
extra, 48
eyes, 160
eyne (Sh.), **160**

façade, 58
faerie (Spenser), **161**
fairy, 167
fakir, 78
fall (Amer.), 82, **190**
fall of leaf (Sh.), 82
far (Spenser), 103
farre (Spenser), 103
fascism, 84
fat, 121
father'd (Sh.), 161
faucet (Amer.), **190**
favour, 58, 154
feel (Amer.), **192**
fell, 122
fellow, 66
fiancée, 60
fichu, 60
filibuster (Amer.), 81
find, 208
fin-de-siècle, 60
fiord, 67
fix (Amer.), **192**
focus, 48
folk-wain (Barnes), 83
fond, 122
fondant, 60
forbidden, 171
forbidd'n (Milton), 171
foregone conclusion (Sh.), 148, **163**
forlorn hope, 71, **207**
forte, 59
foul (Milton), 103
frame-up (Amer.), **193**
franc-tireur, 60
freebooter, 70
Frenchify, 116
fricassée, 59

full of grace, **154**
fungus, 48
furlough, 70
fuselage, 61
fusillade, 60

galore, 75
gape, 67
garage, 58, **61**
garble, 78
gâteau, 55
gauche, 60
gauntlet, 67, **68**
gawk, 122
gawky, 122
gazelle, 79
geisha, 79
genius, 48
get, **190**
ghost, 95
ghoul, 78
ghoulish, 78
glad tidings, **154**
glen, 75
gloomy, **160**
gondola, 73
Gospel, 41
gotten (Amer.), **190**
goulash, 77
grace, 15
grandee, 74
graph, 49
gratin, 60
groove, 70
group, 59
grovelling, 121
guarantee, 55
guardian, 55
guillotine, 60

habitué, 60
hallow, 57
handbook, **83**
hangar, 61
hanker, 71
happy (Sh.), **161**
happy-valiant (Sh.), 161

hara-kiri, 80
harem, 78
harmony, 50
has, 121
hate, 35
hath, 121
he, 142, (Milton), 171
heap, 71
heaven (Milton), 171
heav'n (Milton), 171
hee (Milton), 171
hepatic, 51
her, 45, 142
highly-favoured, **154**
him, 137, 142
hit, 66, 118
hobble, 70
hoist, 70
honest, 125
honesty, 125
honoris causa, 116
honour, 58
hookah, 78
hop, 70
hors-de-combat, 60
houri, 78
house-dweller, 66
housel (Sh.), 31
humaneness, 50
husband, 66
hustings, 66
hustle, 71
hyper-, 50
hyper-sensitive, 51
hyphen, 50

I, 142
iambs, 46
-ic, 48
igloo, 80
ignoramus, 48
iland (Milton), 171
ill, 67
imam, 78
impasse, 61
incarnadine (Sh.), 160

index, 43
indict, 104
indigo, 59
inertia, 48
inferno, 73
infra dig., 116
infra-red, 50
-ing, 142
inscape (Hopkins), 180
insomnia, 48
instress (Hopkins), 180
intelligentsia, 76
intermission, 81
-ion, 116
irksome, 122
irony, 50
island, 171

jasmin, 79
juggernaut, 79
jujitsu, 80
just, 116

khaki, 79
kimono, 80
kindergarten, 68
knight, 125
kowtow, 80

L.S.D., 161
labour, 84, 120
lake, 58
landscape, 70
larynx, 50
lascar, 79
law, 66
lead, 126
legitimate, 43
lens, 48
lèse majesté, 54
liaison, 59
like, 115
likeable, 115
limousine, 61
liqueur, 60

littérateur, 60
loan, 67
loch, 75
loiter, 70
Lond of Faerie (Spenser), 167
longing, 35
lorgnette, 60
love, 19, 35, 94, 154
love-scape (Hopkins), 180
loving kindness, 152

macabre, 60
machine, 59, (Amer.), 193
Madonna, 73
madrasah, 78
madrigal, 73
maelstrom, 67
magazine, 78
Magdalen, 105
Magyar, 77
malfeasance, 54
mammoth, 76
mandarin, 75
manequin, 71
mangelwurzel, 68
manikin, 70, 71
manœuvre, 60
manual, 83
markword of such-ness, 83
marline, 70
marmalade, 74
Mass, 38
matinée, 60
maudlin, 105
may, 139
me, 45, 137, 142, (Milton), 171
mediator, 43
medium, 48
mee (Milton), 171
memento, 43
menage, 58
mendacious, 115

-ment, 115
menu, 60
mere, 125
merriment, 115
merry, 115, 133
mess of pottage, 151, 152
metaphor, 105
métier, 59
mica, 19
might, 94, 139
mill, 37
mind, 208
minimum, 48
minster, 38
minx, 70
mirk, 121
miser, 48
mob, 116
mobled (Sh.), 157
mobocracy, 117
mongoose, 79
monk, 39, 94
moratorium, 48
mosquito, 74
motif, 60
mouse, 19
mousse, 60
moustache, 59
murky, 121
museum, 50
muslin, 59

-n (Milton), 171
nabob, 79
naïve, 59
naughty, 125
nawab, 79
need, 115
needment (Spenser), 115
négligé, 60
neurology, 51
nitwit, 71, 72
not-to-be-thought-uponable (Pecock), 36

noun, 41
nuance, 60
nucleus, 48
nymph, 50

O.K., 81
-ocracy, 117
odium, 35
-ology, 51
opus, 48
orangutang, 80
-ose, 115
otiose, 115
-ous, 115
outlaw, 66
oyez, 54

pagoda, 75
pandæmonium,
    (Milton), 173
pandemonium, 50,
    (Milton), 173, 175
paprika, 77
par excellence, 59
parole, 59
parquet, 60
parterre, 59
participle, 41
partisan, 59
party machine
    (Amer.), 192
passé, 60
pass out (Amer.), 193
past praying for
    (Sh.), 163
pathos, 50
patience on a monu-
    ment (Sh.), 148
pauper, 43
peace, 58
peak (Sh.), 159
peaky, 159
pedestrian, 83
penchant, 59
pendulum, 48
perceive, 192

peripatetic, 49
phase, 50
pheeze (Sh.), 158
phenomenal, 49
philander, 50
phlebotomy, 51
phone, 49
phonograph, 49
piazza, 73
pibroch, 75
picnic, 60
picture, 199
pilaster, 73
pilgrim, 73
pilot, 59
pine (Sh.), 159
piquant, 59
plaid, 75
plaintif, 54
plunder, 68
police, 60, 118
politician (Amer.),
    191
portière, 60
post, 115
poste restante, 60
post-war, 50, 115
potato, 74, 80
pother, 122
pre-, 115
première, 60
preposition, 41
presently (Sh.), 108,
    124
prestige, 61
pre-war, 115
priest, 38, 154
prima donna, 73
privilege, 54
Prodigal son, 151
profile, 60
promenade, 59
prosecutor, 116
proviso, 43
psychology, 51
pull, 193
pylon, 50

quart, 59
quean, 127
queen, 127

raconteur, 60
radio, 83, 118
ragged, 66
raiment, 153
raison d'être, 61
ransack, 67
rapacious, 115
rapprochement, 61
rathe (Milton), 174
ration, 118
read, 126
reason, 58
recipe, 116
red, 76, 126
referendum, 48
régime, 60
Renaissance, 60
rendez-vous, 59
renegade, 74
replica, 73
reprimand, 59
requiem, 43
requisition, 116
restaurant, 60
resumé, 60
reticule, 60
revue, 61
rid, 115
riddance, 115
ride, 118
Riding, 67
right, 94, 115
righteous, 115
risqué, 60
rissole, 60
robot, 76
rococo, 60
rook, 79
root, 66
rosette, 60
roué, 60
rouge, 60
run, 118

-s (third person singular), 121
-s (genitive), 136
sable, 76
safe (Sh.), 161
saffron, 78
saga, 67
sago, 80
sahib, 79
saint, 57
salad days (Sh.), 148
sally, 59
salon, 60
same, 67
sauté, 60
savoir faire, 60
scapegoat, 151, 152
Schottische, 68
scot free, 67
scrannel (Milton), 174
scribe, 43
Scripture, 57
seal, 178
senior, 154
sense (Amer.), 82, 192
seraglio, 73
set, 120
shale, 68
shampoo, 79
shamrock, 75
shanghai, 118
shawl, 79
she, 142, 171
shee (Milton), 171
should, 139
siesta, 74
simile, 43
skald, 67
ski, 67
skill, 67
skin, 66
skipper, 70
sky, 67
sloop, 70
slumber, 178

snare, 66
socialism, 84
sociology, 51
solicitor (Amer.), 191
son, 59, 94
sortie, 60
soufflé, 60
soul (Milton), 103
soup, 59
sovereign, 171
Soviet, 76, 132
sovietize, 132
sovran (Milton), 171
spade, 74
spaghetti, 73
spaniel'd (Sh.), 161
speak within door (Sh.), 159
species, 48
splice, 70
splint, 70
spook (Amer.), 72
spool, 70
sporran, 75
squaw, 80
stanza (Sh.), 73
status, 48, 115
status quo ante, 115
stevedore, 74
stiletto, 73
still, 125
stockade, 59
stratum, 118
street, 37
studio, 73
suède, 60
swabber, 70
sweat of thy brow, 152
syrop, 78

-t (Milton), 171
table, 57, 58
tableau, 59
taboo, 80
take, 66
tap, 190

tattoo, 80, 118
tea, 80
teeth, 19
telegram, 83
telephone, 49
tender-hearted, 152
-th, 121
that, 91, 139–141
the, 91
theatre, 50
thee, 137
their, 64, 66, 137, (Milton), 171
them, 64, 66, 137
theory, 50
therm, 50
they, 64, 66, 137
thir (Milton), 171
thou, 137
thrall, 66
tolerance, 49
tooth, 19
torpor, 48
tort, 54
tragedy, 50
trap (Sh.), 158
trespasses, 151
tricolor, 60
Trinity, 41
trochees, 46
troll, 67
tropically (Sh.), 158
try conclusions (Sh.), 163
tungsten, 68
tyrant, 50

ugly, 67, 122
ultimatum, 48
un- (Sh.), 161
unaneal'd (Sh.), 31
unavoided (Sh.), 161
unbless (Sh.), 161
unbody (Sh.), 161
uncharge (Sh.), 162
uncolted (Sh.), 162

unexpressive (Sh.), 162
unfather'd (Sh.), 162
unfellowed (Sh.), 162
ungot (Sh.), 162
ungothroughsome (Pecock), 36
unhair (Sh.), 162
unhousel'd (Sh.), 31
unjust, 116
unkiss (Sh.), 162
unpropitious, 50
unroosted (Sh.), 162
unvalued (Sh.), 161
uproar, 71
urge, 66

vacuum, 48
vagary, 48
valet, 58
vamoose (Amer.), 74
vapour, 116
vapourish, 116
vase, 59
vat, 121
veldt, 72

vendetta, 73
verbose, 115
vers libre, 61
verve, 59
via, 48
victuals, 104
viewpoint (Amer.), 82
viking, 67
villainous, 115
virtue, 58
vixen, 121
volcano, 73
volley, 59
vulgar, 125

waggon, 71
walker, 83
want, 67
warden, 55
warrant, 55
wastel, 55
weak, 67
what the dickens (Sh.), 147, 162
which, 140, 141

whisky, 75
who, 46, 139–142
whom, 46, 139–142
whose, 140, 141
wind, 208
wine-fat, 121
wing, 67
wire, 83
wireless, 83
wit, 116
witticism, 116
wolfram, 68
word, 5
would, 139
Writ, 57
wrong, 66

yashmak, 78
yat, 91
ye, 91, 137
yodel, 68
you, 137

zeitgeist, 68
zenith, 78
zero, 78